DISCI-PLESHIP PROJECT

Lucas Leys
David Noboa

DISCI-PLESHIP PROJECT

Lucas Leys
David Noboa

e625.com

DISCIPLESHIP PROJECT – HIGH SCHOOL MINISTRY
e625 - 2024
Dallas, Texas
e625 ©2024 by **Lucas Leys y David Noboa**

____

All Bible verses are from the New International Version (NIV) unless otherwise specified.

Translated by: Josiah Brown

Interior Design and Cover: JuanShimabukuroDesign

ISBN: 978-1-954149-55-7

PRINTED IN THE UNITED STATES OF AMERICA

CONTENTS

INTRO 7

SESSION 1

ESSENTIAL PRINCIPLES OF BIBLICAL DISCIPLESHIP 15

   1. WE ARE THE CHURCH 17

   2. TEACHING AND DISCIPLESHIP ARE NOT THE SAME THING 23

   3. EVERY DISCIPLE IS DIFFERENT 27

   4. DISCIPLESHIP IS FOR EVERY AGE .31

   5. DISCIPLESHIP HAPPENS IN PROCESSES 35

   6. ACCOMPANIMENT AND MENTORSHIP 39

   7. PARENTS' INVOLVEMENT 43

   8. THE MIRROR PRINCIPLE 47

   9. ACTIVITIES WITH A PURPOSE 51

  10. THE CALL IS FOR EVERYONE 55

SESSION 2

10 LESSONS FOR DISCIPLING TEENS 59

   1. THE ROLLER COASTER OF EMOTIONS 63

   2. IDENTITY AND SELF-ESTEEM 75

   3. INTERNAL EXPLOSIONS 87

   4. DREAMS OF ATTRACTION 99

5. SEXUAL INTELLIGENCE 113

6. THE FUNDAMENTAL CONNECTION .125

7. ROMANCE AND DATING 137

8. HEALTHY RELATIONSHIPS 149

9. SPIRITUAL NARCISSISM 159

10. BOUNDARIES AND FREEDOM 171

BIBLIOGRAPHY 185

INTRO

Success is only a consequence of having developed discipline with perseverance.

Lucas Leys, *Stamina*

In the Bible we find the story of when Jesus, after his resurrection, had an encounter with two of his disciples while they were walking toward Emmaus, a city located 10 kilometers from Jerusalem. As we read in this story from Luke chapter 24, those who claimed to be his followers did not know, at that moment, who he was. Doesn't that statement intrigue you? How is it that those who recognized themselves as his followers could not recognize him? The answers can be many. Some illustrate Jesus hidden behind a cloak, others say that his glorified image was different from his human form previous to the crucifixion, or perhaps he had the ability to confuse people's eyes so that they did not recognize him. The truth is that they did not know who he was until the moment he broke the bread and only then could they recognize him.

Whatever the explanation, the story highlights a powerful truth: It is not enough to know who Jesus is. Jesus can walk with you without you being able to recognize him, and suddenly, poof! a great revelation comes into your life that makes you see clearly that Jesus has been walking and talking with you the whole time.

THAT IS THE TASK OF THE DISCIPLERS: WALK WITH SOMEONE SO THEY CAN CLEARLY SEE JESUS.

That is the task of disciplers: walk with someone so that they can clearly see Jesus; accompanying another who still cannot recognize him in certain aspects of their life. And that is the challenge of biblical discipleship: traveling with another person until they can recognize the Messiah, their inner blindfolds drop, and they experience the presence of God through the risen Christ.

WHAT DISCIPLESHIP IS NOT

On many occasions, the clearest way to define something is to list what it is not, and here is a list of what biblical discipleship is not

- **IT IS NOT A BIBLE CLASS.** Usually, these two expressions get confused with each other since they often go hand in hand, but they are not the same. Teaching the Bible is an indispensable part of discipleship and that is why this book contains lessons to teach. However, this book includes the word *project* because just teaching a Bible class is not the whole of discipleship.

- **IT IS NOT A MEMBERSHIP PROGRAM.** In some churches it is believed that discipleship is an initiation program for new believers. We want new believers to start being disciples of Jesus and it is great that there is a good program for those who are taking their first steps in faith. But discipleship does not end with baptism or with the completion of a course. It is not about attending a series of workshops. Although these can help a lot in the discipleship process, you will see that biblical knowledge and other types of learning do not necessarily result in greater spiritual maturity.

- **IT IS NOT A DOCTRINAL REFLECTION.** Discipleship is not limited to intellectual matters. Rather, it is a process of integral character development that involves, in addition to the brain, the spirit, emotions, will, and conduct. Theology classes could make us fall into the delusion that by learning certain doctrines, we will be good disciples. The doctrines, of course, are fundamental and there is doctrinal teaching in true biblical discipleship, but those doctrines must be put into action to have an effect. Knowing theology and doctrine does not make you a good disciple if it does not lead to a tangible practice. Consider, for example, the Pharisees, whom Jesus was confronting. They had a lot of knowledge, and they handled theology and doctrine perfectly, but their hearts were far from God.

GENUINE DISCIPLESHIP IS MORE LIKE BEING A MIRROR OF CHRIST THAN SIMPLY TEACHING ABOUT HIM.

- **IT IS NOT A LITURGY.** Although it is. It is true that discipleship has a lot to do with acquiring good habits and spiritual disciplines, these things should not become cold repetitions or rigid religious behavior. Each discipline acquired, each moment of collective worship, each act of community participation, prayer, and fasting, are tools for our hearts to be conquered by the heart of Jesus and not only for us to "do" what is right in the eyes of others.

One can know a lot about God and be far from him, and because of this, genuine discipleship is more like being a mirror of Christ than simply teaching about him.

The point is not to "show" who is more like Jesus but to be clear that the more I focus on willingly reflecting Christ, the better discipler I will be.

So, what is biblical discipleship? Putting together just one sentence that includes all that genuine discipleship means can be very daring. . . but we can try:

**CHRISTIAN DISCIPLESHIP IS A PROCESS OF ACCOMPANIMENT }
IN WHICH, THROUGH A PERSONAL RELATIONSHIP,
SOMEONE IS ABLE TO FACILITATE IN THE DISCIPLE THE VIRTUES
OF THE CHARACTER OF JESUS.**

THINK OF THESE TWO WORDS

- **PROCESS:** Discipleship is a progressive and patient process. It has to do with accompanying a person from one place to another, just as it happened with the travelers in Emmaus. As they walked, Jesus reminded them of things they had already heard and told them things they did not yet know. And they lived the "process" of that walk with such intensity that when they finally realized it was their Master, they remembered that their hearts burned while he spoke to them.

- **RELATIONSHIP:** Discipleship does not happen without accompaniment. Walking together with someone means "being there" for that person. It's not just about giving lessons or classes, and it needs to be more than just a weekly meeting. Discipleship goes beyond being together for church services or scheduled meetings. The best disciplers share other moments of life with their apprentices and that is why the lessons in this book will challenge you to move from the lesson into community. That's how Jesus did it. And that is how we will do it.

THE MORE I FOCUS ON VOLUNTARILY REFLECTING CHRIST, THE BETTER DISCIPLER I WILL BE.

The twelve disciples were not the only followers of Jesus, but they were the most intimate. Throughout the time that our Messiah walked among human beings, many were close to him and that is still true today. Do you remember the crowd eating freely of the loaves and fishes?

There may be many followers of Jesus, but not all who claim to follow him are truly his disciples.

The Bible says that the Word became flesh and dwelt among us. He lived with men proclaiming that the kingdom of heaven had drawn near. He died. He rose again. And just before leaving to return to the throne prepared for him, he left a great task: *Go and make disciples, teach them to observe all the things that I have told you.* Then it is said that more than 500 people witnessed the ascension of the Savior (1 Corinthians 15:6).

The great task of making disciples of all nations is being carried out with various nuances, and in initiating this project in our churches, the imperative question to answer is: How can we make better disciples of Jesus?

As you go through this book, you will be given 10 crucial premises about the different aspects that biblical discipleship represents. Beyond the transmission of knowledge, these premises are intended to help you in the transmission of a CULTURE. That is what Christ came to establish: the culture of the kingdom of heaven, the precise interpretation of what the Father had said since ancient times, the social exercise of a people, which we now call family, and the characteristics that this family must have. As you can see, these are valuable things that we cannot forget.

Jesus announced that he had come to fulfill the law and not to abolish it, but he did not teach his disciples a series of steps to be better believers. He lived a lifestyle of faith with them. Jesus was with his disciples even in the most difficult moments, but he did not gather them together to give them a talk on obedience. He obeyed the Father in everything, and thus taught them to do the same.

> *This is the covenant I will make with them after that time, says the Lord. I will put my laws in their hearts, and I will write them on their minds.*
>
> (Hebrews 10:16)

PRIOR TRAINING FOR DISCIPLERS

Your church and ministry can do transformational discipleship and this preliminary training is intended to:

- Break any incorrect paradigm that exists around biblical discipleship in the understanding of your team members.

- Excite and encourage your volunteers with the challenging and wonderful project of making your participants more like Jesus.

- Optimize the growth process by establishing clear results for your ministry.

- Expand the vision of all those involved, recovering the sense of community of the first-century church.

ESSENTIAL PRINCIPLES OF BIBLICAL DISCIPLESHIP

WE ARE THE CHURCH

The greatest gift a church can receive is to have a group of families who take their responsibilities with such Christian seriousness that they are willing to completely alter their lifestyle to raise up disciples for Jesus Christ.

Abraham Kuyper

For a long time, we got so used to having meetings in a temple as part of the natural exercise of the church that this inertia produced in us a forgetfulness. We forgot we must be and make disciples, and not just attend meetings. In a biblical sense, the church is not a place to go, but a family to belong to, and if we fail to see it in this way, we will end up stunting our personal growth and that of the church.

The way we speak exhibits how we think and, consequently, how we act. Look at this conversation.

—What church do you go to?

—I attend Central Church.

—But... are you one of those who serve?

— I only attend, I am not in any ministry.

THE CHURCH IS NOT A PLACE TO GO, BUT A FAMILY TO BELONG TO.

Surely you heard something similar. But the truth is that "attending" an ecclesial community is practically impossible from God's perspective. Think of your family.

Do you attend your family weekly or are you part of it? Being part of the church and congregating is not the same as attending.

A biblical answer to the above question would be:

—I do not attend a church; I *am* the church of Christ.

Another very common comment is the following:

—I didn't go to church this week.

And their leader replies: —Well, you shouldn't miss it because remember we shouldn't stop congregating.

Nobody has bad intentions when saying these things but doing so can push the new generations to lead a double life. What exactly is congregate? Obviously, the word means to come together but in a biblical sense it means to be linked. Share a feeling, a belief, and a practical coexistence.

SAYING "WE ARE THE CHURCH" LETS US KNOW THAT WE ARE PART OF THE CHURCH AND WE WILL NEVER STOP BEING SO.

We must avoid having on one side of life: church meetings in which everyone is good, helpful, and even a good example for others, while having on the other side the "secular life." We have lived in that dichotomy for centuries, and it is time to say that it is wrong and that it is not biblical because, according to the written Word, there is no Christian life and secular life. If you are a disciple of Jesus then you are in whatever place, moment, condition, and activity; and everything you do you must do for the Lord (Colossians 3:23-24).

The phrase "go to church" makes us think that it is a destination to visit, a good place to hang out on certain days of the week. Instead, saying "we are the church" lets us know that we are a part of the church, and we never stop being so, no matter where we are or whom we are with.

Look at the following text from your Bible:

> The God who made the world and everything in it is the Lord of heaven and earth and does not live in temples built by human hands. And he is not served by human hands, as if he needed anything. Rather, he himself gives everyone life and breath and everything else. From one man he made all the nations, that they should inhabit the whole earth; and he marked out their appointed times in history and the boundaries of their lands. God did this so that they would seek him and perhaps reach out for him and find him, though he is not far from any one of us. "For in him we live and move and have our being". As some of your own poets have said, "We are his offspring."
> (Acts 17:24-28)

God is not always in the temples, but he is always in the church.

Many find it difficult to understand this phrase because they consider the temple as a synonym for church, but it is not. We are the church! What verse 28 says is compelling: "'For in him we live and move and have our being.' As some of your own poets have said, 'We are his offspring.'" God is in the church, so he dwells in us, and we are a part of his family.

GOD IS NOT ALWAYS IN THE TEMPLES, BUT HE IS ALWAYS IN THE CHURCH.

We gather in temples, yes, but God is not there because of the place; he is there because of us, his church. True disciples never cease to be the church and that is precisely why they are aware that they must be an active part of the meetings. They know how important community life is, they are a part of the body, they relate to others, and they serve God with their gifts and talents. But their mission does not end there. The disciple looks inside themself, examines themself periodically, and renders an account to their discipler based on the growth steps that the individual has taken. For this reason, although one participates in the meetings, **a disciple does not depend on the meeting to grow and fulfill what Christ has entrusted to them.**

Attending a congregation does not require you to be a disciple but BEING PART of a community of followers of Jesus requires you to be a disciple wherever you are, and requires you to fulfill the mission of making other disciples! No matter what community of believers you belong to, the mission remains the same, and you remain a part of the global church. We are all united in the same faith, purpose, and mission.

This perspective is born from understanding that the church is not a place limited to a physical space, but is a living organism and, as such, must grow integrally, as well as reproduce, multiply, and expand. If this does not happen, it is because we are doing something wrong.

Remember that just being a disciple of Jesus is not God's complete plan for you. It is also necessary to make disciples, model the character of Christ to others, accompany them to live this process, and encourage them to duplicate themselves in others.

PARADIGM SHIFTS

- I do not attend a church; I AM the church.

- The building where we meet is NOT the church, it is a temple.

- The church is not a static place; it is a LIVING organism.

- The church is made up of the children of God, wherever they come together. Whether that's in a large auditorium, in a park, or in a house, wherever the children of God are, that is where the church is.

IMPLEMENT IDEAS THAT CHANGE THE CULTURE

- Put up posters in the temple with phrases that help everyone change their mindset from "going to church" to "being the church."

- Try to repeat these phrases several times in meetings until the concepts become part of the habitual language.

- Work with all ministry members and volunteers so that in classes, small group meetings, and even individual counseling it is clearly stated that everything we Christians do every day has to do with the church.

TEACHING AND DISCIPLESHIP ARE NOT THE SAME THING

A Christian understanding of the world sees a child´s character not as genetically determined but as shaped to a significant degree by parental discipleship and discipline.

Russell D. Moore

It is easy to mix up teaching and discipleship because teaching is part of discipleship, but it is essential to differentiate between them. While discipleship uses teaching, teaching alone does not make disciples.

The practical reality of today's Christians is that we are bombarded by an enormous amount of diverse information, messages, and teachings on multiple networks. We have everything, and we idolize those who "speak better" and have popular social followings, but. . . how are we making disciples? Obviously, we don't want to judge anyone's character, but it's good to be clear that speaking well for a limited amount of time in a video or on a stage is not the same as doing what Jesus commanded us to do. Discipling is more than just speaking well.

Perhaps the key is not to stay in the discursive part of communication. Both authors of this book worked on this material because we want to help you include personal challenges in your teaching and in that intentional process which we are calling discipleship.

The personal or collective challenges that put into practice what has been learned in a relationship optimize results.

Reflect with your team on these differences between teaching and discipleship:

TEACHING	DISCIPLESHIP
Transmits knowledge.	Transmits a culture.
Is limited to classes and does not require much of a relationship with the teacher.	Aims for accompaniment and requires a relationship with the discipler.
Is based on knowing what the Bible or theology says.	Is based on practicing what the Bible says.
Leads you to greater knowledge.	Leads you to maturity in Christ.
Is a short moment or stage of life aimed to finish a program, training, or class.	Is a process that focuses on one's character.

If you pay attention to this chart, you can see that discipleship takes much more effort and time than teaching. Teachers are a key part of the process, but if you really want to disciple others, you are going to have to move to a new level of commitment and relationship. The process can start with teaching, but it doesn't end there.

WHOEVER EXERCISES THE INTENTIONAL PROCESS OF DISCIPLESHIP ASSUMES TRAITS OF SPIRITUAL PATERNITY.

Can you be a teacher and not be making disciples? Yes. When you limit teaching to the imparting of information, then the Word becomes a theory, and that conformism prevents God's truth from being real and alive in the person's life.

When you understand this and change the way you teach, then everything you teach will bear more fruit, since it will point toward the goal of making disciples and not just creating clones that know everything you already know. Additionally, at the end of the road, we are sure that you will be taught by each disciple too, because you never stop being one!

Someone who disciples is much more than a teacher. Little by little they become an example of life, a counselor, a coach, and a friend. Whoever exercises the intentional process of discipleship assumes traits of spiritual paternity since they assign identity, provide, and protect.

PARADIGM SHIFTS

- Teaching is not the "whole point" of discipleship.

- The driving force of discipleship is the relationships, not the knowledge.

- Knowing the Bible does not bring maturity; living it does.

IMPLEMENT IDEAS THAT CHANGE THE CULTURE

- Begin to differentiate biblical classes from discipleship processes.

- Instruct all involved (leaders, volunteers, and participants) to understand the difference.

- Identify those in your congregation who can be disciplers and train them with this guide.

- Make sure that all classes point to changes of action that will be monitored in a relationship.

EVERY DISCIPLE IS DIFFERENT

Fortunately, God made all varieties of people with a wide variety of interests and abilities. He has called people of every race and color who have been hurt by life in every manner imaginable. Even the scars of past abuse and injury can be the means of bringing healing to another. What wonderful opportunities to make disciples!

Charles R. Swindoll

The Greek philosophy that we inherited in the West from the Roman Empire gave us the not-so-astute idea that education should be like a funnel through which we all go in differently and then we all come out the same. Some have unknowingly sought this type of approach for discipleship and the church.

For this reason, programs are created with the expectation that every believer can complete them and become the same as all other Christians. However, today it is clear that we are all the same in essence, but we are all unique and we must all be brought to discipleship. Recognizing this is a good thing! Every disciple is different, has specific needs, and struggles with things that others don't. Their strengths and weaknesses are unique, and it is not possible to create a program that can serve everyone equally.

EVERY DISCIPLE IS DIFFERENT, HAS SPECIFIC NEEDS, AND STRUGGLES WITH THINGS THAT OTHERS DON'T.

In turn, the disciplers are aware of their own weaknesses in order to depend more on Christ, assume their strengths to be imparted to their followers, and are all fully guided by the Spirit of God.

It is for this reason that discipleship is more about personal development than just a collective group development. The group and the individual must be two complementary parts because it is not one or the other but both. There are truths that are better learned communally and others that must be taught face-to-face in the intimacy of two people. The challenge is that almost all church programs are made up of a big or small collective of people and there is little one-on-one approach. This is why it is so vital to remember that intimate conversations, personal encounters, and one-on-one challenges are a mark of genuine discipleship.

Some ideas to disciple on a personal level:

- Don't look at numbers, look at people.

- Create opportunities that go outside of a class setting.

- Create appropriate intentional intimacy as opposed to waiting for it to come naturally.

- Find out the interests of each disciple.

- If you want a genuine relationship, be authentic.

- Invest more into those who show greater interest and enthusiasm.

- Teach them to be accountable for their lives. This is imperative.

- Celebrate their successes; comfort them in their setbacks.

- Work on specific actions.

- Help them set/focus on personal goals.

- Assist them in depending on the Holy Spirit to be their guide.

These tips will vary slightly if you are discipling children, preteens, teens, or young adults. Each of the following principles will assist you in discovering the superior point of focus for each of the age groups. There is, however, no age limitation for someone to become a disciple.

PARADIGM SHIFTS

- To God we are all equal, but we are also different and unique.

- Discipleship always becomes a personal relationship.

- The weekly meetings do not disciple; the relationship does.

- We were created in the image and likeness of a multiform God.

IMPLEMENT IDEAS THAT CHANGE THE CULTURE

- Know the individual differences of the people who are in your discipleship group.

- Intentionally be aware of which paradigm is important to transfer value to them.

- Help the people you disciple get to know each other better.

- Create a conscious awareness of inclusion and integration in the members of your discipleship projects.

- Model a personalized pastoral approach.

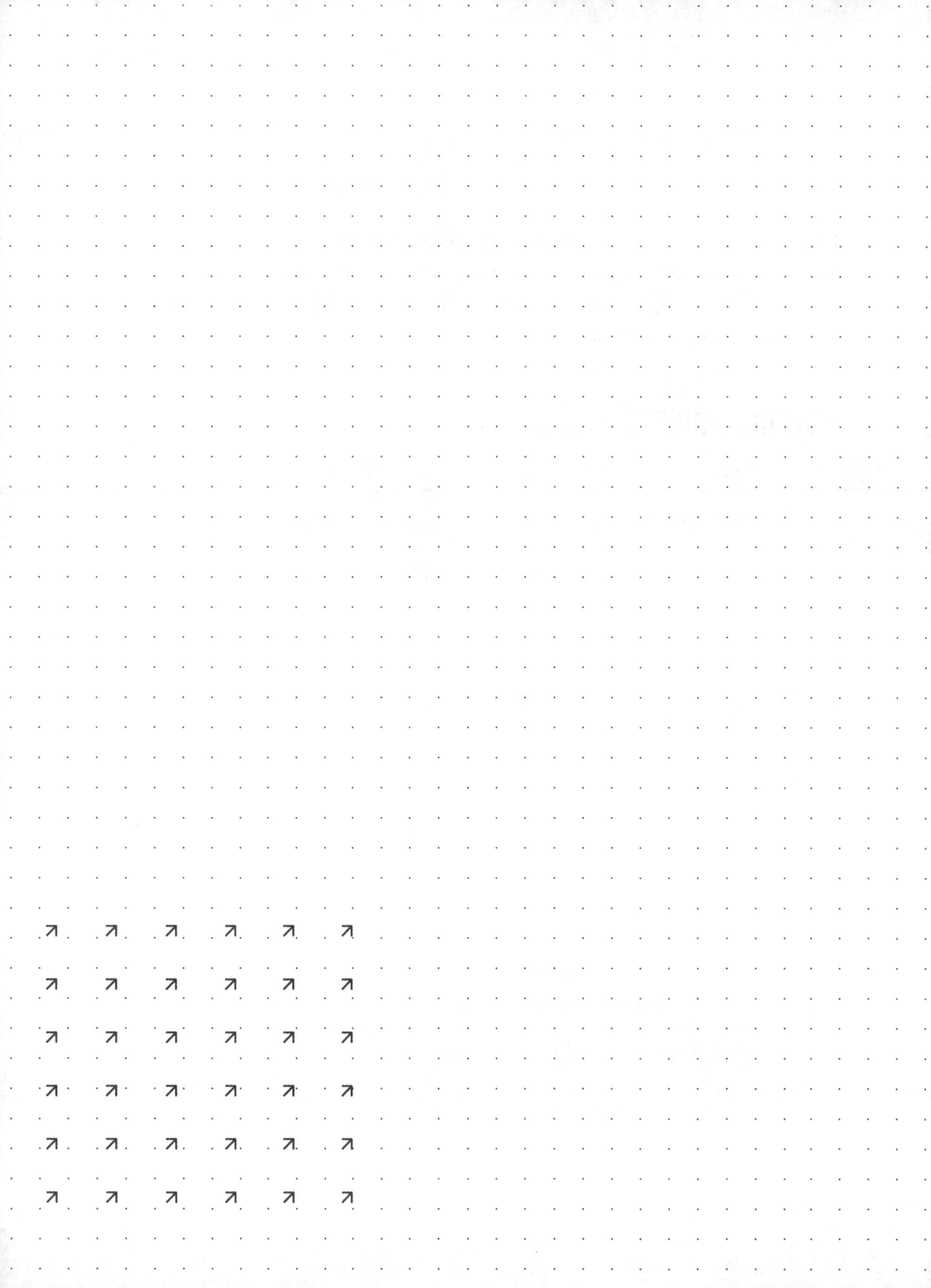

DISCIPLESHIP IS FOR EVERY AGE

Jesus spent time and had close and personal relationships with his disciples. Do we have personal relationships with the new generations in our churches?

La Verne Tolbert

It seems that the general conscience of many congregations demands that we "seriously" disciple adults, while children, preteens, teens, and young adults can wait, and this is a strategic error with dire consequences. In fact, when it comes to transmitting culture, the best age is the youngest. When you work with adults you will find that it is a little more difficult to change something that they have done in a certain and determined way for their entire lives. Instead, the youngest are moldable, teachable, and adaptable. They know that they don't know, and that's good.

If you have an influential position with the new generations, God has held you in high esteem.

Now, working with children is not the same as working with young adults, so here are some recommendations that correspond to the 4 basic work areas of an intelligent vision for generational pastoral care.

WHEN IT COMES TO TRANSMITTING CULTURE, THE BEST AGE IS THE YOUNGEST.

FOR THE DISCIPLESHIP OF CHILDREN

- Work closely with parents. They are the natural leaders and disciplers that God gave children. Discipling children is cooperating with their parents.

- Help children share their growth steps in the context of their family.

- Use multiple sources, so the training process will be comprehensive and will reach everyone. (If you want to know more about multiple intelligences, take advantage of the course at the e625 online Institute.)

FOR THE DISCIPLESHIP OF PRETEENS

- This is the stage where we begin to see the world beyond just the home and with the arrival of abstract thought we begin to question the validity of what we learned in childhood. For this reason, teaching must move from concrete data to abstract principles.

- At this stage it is also crucial to collaborate with their parents because this is the last great opportunity they will have to shape desired values and habits in their children. In the following stages of their lives, instilling values becomes more difficult.

- The relationship with their leaders and teachers must now be more personal. They need models and it is very possible that the models they have at this stage will continue to subconsciously be their example for the rest of their lives.

FOR THE DISCIPLESHIP OF TEENS

- The relationship of boys and girls with their parents is always important, but the relationship with their friends at this age is key. Communal discipleship is most significant at this stage.

- Naturally, in adolescence we all question our family framework and leaders should not throw more fuel on the fire but rather help them positively make that evaluation.

- Be prepared to talk with them about feelings and emotions. Their life during this stage is going to be a roller coaster of emotional ups and downs and they will need someone mature, and therefore stable, to accompany them.

FOR THE DISCIPLESHIP OF YOUNG ADULTS

- To the same degree that communal discipleship is vital in the previous stage, mentorship is vital in this young adult phase. A mentor meets their deepest needs and allows space to ask difficult questions, even the most intimate questions.

- Present options to young adults without giving them orders and, above all, without making decisions for them. Teach them to make their decisions based on the Word of God. Coaching is a good discipline to add to your skills and in the e625.com online institute you can find foundational generational coaching courses.

- In this stage, most consider pursuing a profession, choosing a marriage partner, planning for the future, and discovering one's life purpose (or even a ministerial calling). These are the talking points in the discipleship relationship with young adults.

PARADIGM SHIFTS

- Age is not a limitation to making disciples, but it is necessary to adapt according to the stage.

- Discipling adults is not more valuable than discipling little ones.

- The transferring of culture takes time, focus, and effort.

IMPLEMENT IDEAS THAT CHANGE THE CULTURE

- Work on a vision of *Generational Leadership.*[1] (If you haven't read this book we recommend you do so as soon as possible.) Join the adult ministries with those in your congregation who are dedicated to the new generations and plan an activity that focuses on making the discipleship of new generations a priority for your entire church, as it was commissioned by God in Deuteronomy 6. Coordinating efforts from time to time does wonders for the heart and minds of co-laborers.

- Organize things in a way that each of the new generational stages leads a meeting one or more times per year. Give preteens responsibilities, encourage teens to be an example for the little ones, train young adults to model behavior in teens, and provide examples of maturity to take firm steps toward the next stage in which they find themselves.

---

[1]. Lucas Leys, *Liderazgo Generacional.* (Dallas, Texas: Editorial e625, 2017).

DISCIPLESHIP HAPPENS IN PROCESSES

When the church becomes an end in itself, it ends. When any ministry, no matter how great, becomes an end goal, it ends. What we need is for discipleship to become the goal, and then the process of conversion and sanctification will never end.
Robby Gallaty

When we talk about discipling others, we must consider how to elevate our disciples' level of maturity. It is about going from one point to the next. This makes it necessary to draw a route that marks the steps of that sustained growth that we seek, while understanding that there are smaller steps along the way. When we understand this better, we focus less on our own assessment of events and pay more attention to a progressive view of processes.

It is one thing to learn a principle and quite another to live it. The first is an intellectual act, something that can be received in a class. To put a principle into practice, however, requires decision, effort, and the fulfillment of goals that help make the principle a part of our culture and way of life.

For this reason, someone who decides to disciple cannot be satisfied with teaching principles, since that is only the first part. It is necessary that these principles

WE FOCUS LESS ON OUR OWN ASSESSMENT OF EVENTS AND PAY MORE ATTENTION TO A PROGRESSIVE VIEW OF PROCESSES.

are part of the discipler's culture so that they can transmit them in such a way that they become part of the culture of the disciple.

It is a lifestyle that should arise naturally and not be forced.

THE PENTAGON OF LEARNING APPLIED TO DISCIPLESHIP

The book *Generational Leadership* describes the need to improve teaching methods from a relational nuance with the following pentagon:

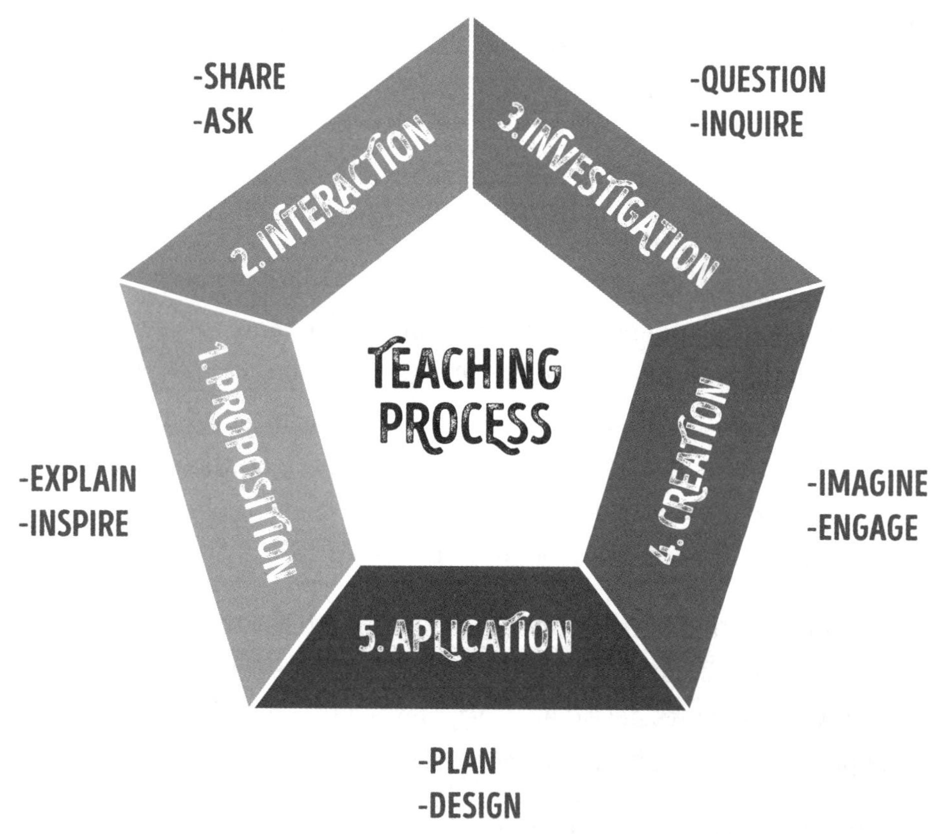

© 2017 Lucas Leys

Each one of the sides of the pentagon marks a dimension of the action that the disciplers must observe. If you think about it well, you will understand the need to make disciples through processes, instead of just having students in a class.

Here's an example of how this process works:

1. **PROPOSITION:** Pick an aspect of the character of Christ.

2. **INTERACTION:** Explore the different appreciations of the aspect.

3. **INVESTIGATION:** Look up what the Bible says about it.

4. **CREATION:** Engage others in doing it together.

5. **APLICATION:** Live it in your own flesh and be accountable for it.

A process can be focused on a specific area of the disciple's life, on a specific theme, on an aspect of character, etc., In this way you can create different proposals for stages that adapt to the principles of this pentagon. Nothing is rigid. On the contrary, everything is adaptable and 100 percent improvable and you can read more in the book *Generational Leadership*.

Although this book may appear to speak to the project of making disciples, it is meant as a tool to help guide a long-term process whose final goal is to form the character of Christ in the life of the believer, which is entirely dependent on the relationship between discipler and disciple and their mutual commitment to the process.

PARADIGM SHIFTS

- Discipleship is not a propositional discourse but a process of internalizing truths that respect the different abilities of our brains to learn.

- The preacher shares a monologue, the teacher teaches a class, the discipler accompanies through stages.

- The relationship between disciplers and disciples is the very nature of discipleship.

IMPLEMENT IDEAS THAT CHANGE THE CULTURE

- Get used to creating processes. Preaching or lectures are not as effective in generating understanding for most people. Use series, long-term lessons, and various instances so that different people internalize the contents of what you want them to practice.

- The call is not to have meetings where we stand to sing and then listen to a lecture. Think outside the sanctuary, the classroom, and the speeches given.

ACCOMPANIMENT AND MENTORSHIP

I believe in the transforming power of the Spirit of God and that Jesus can be formed in the life of the new generations. I work from his reality, not from fiction.

Félix Ortiz

According to what we can notice in the New Testament, the apostle Paul would come to a city, preach, and then continue working with a few select believers until he formed in them the character of Christ so that they would then do the same with others. When it was time, he left there but he did not disconnect from them: he continued to give them instructions through his writings.

If we are talking about relationships and processes, we must consider the development of relationships in phases or stages and that is why it is good to include the word project. If we want to form disciples with maturity, who truly reflect the character of Christ, we must first form the attributes of Christ in ourselves and then gradually develop each aspect of our personal commitments, modeling them in the lives of others. Paul said: "Be imitators of me, just as I am of Christ" and this can take years. At the same time, it is advisable to plan it with phases and times, and then release the disciples so that they go and repeat the process with others.

THE GREATEST WEALTH OF DISCIPLESHIP IS IN THE RELATIONSHIP.

The relationship with your disciples can last a lifetime, and they may even perceive you as a spiritual reference, but that does not necessarily mean that the roles are forever and that they will not grow past it. The point is to accompany them in this stage to help them take steps toward maturity they need to take in this period in which they find themselves. This "staying in touch" can use digital tools such as video chats, social media, and similar tools. But the point is to mentor, that is, model to transfer certain vital lessons that must be learned at a stage in life.

Look what the book of Exodus says about God's relationship with Moses. Although Moses could not look directly into the face of God because he would have died, his personal encounter with the Eternal God produced in him a weight of glory that others could not fail to recognize.

The Lord would speak to Moses face to face, as one speaks to a friend. Then Moses would return to the camp, but his young aide Joshua son of Nun did not leave the tent.
(Exodus 33:11)

In other words, being close to a good role model has an impact that sooner or later everyone will notice. Moses was discipled by God, just as all of us can be. This process is based on the relationship we reach with him. In the same way, we can all accompany others in their growth process.

PARADIGM SHIFTS

- There is no discipleship without accompaniment.

- The greatest wealth of discipleship is in the relationship.

- The discipleship relationship can last a lifetime, although roles usually change according to the stages of life.

IMPLEMENT IDEAS THAT CHANGE THE CULTURE

- Take personal time with each person you have in a discipleship group.

- Let the people in your group know aspects of your life that are outside of a weekly class.

- They should keep in mind from early on that one day they will have to disciple others. Thus, the change will not be left alone in your hands, since the responsibility of making disciples belongs to all believers.

- Create dscipleship projects for specific stages of life with measurable results.

PARENTS' INVOLVEMENT

We discipline our children not so that they will make us happy, but so that they will serve Christ as adults. We educate them not so they can have a good job, but to develop them to be the best follower of Jesus that they can be.
Chap Bettis

All Christian parents are involved in the discipleship of their children even if they don't know it or are unintentional about it. The job of every church leader is to make sure parents know this and help them to be intentional about doing it better.

As children grow, their ability and need to relate to other role models also grows. That is where we come in, not as something parallel to the family but rather by joining forces in a collaborative way. The point is that a constant interaction between leadership and parents goes much further than we might suspect. The role of the parents decreases as the children grow older and it is necessary for this to happen, because otherwise, they could never become mature children who effectively serve the kingdom of heaven. But again. . . this is a PROCESS. It could be slow moving, and we must be patient, but that is why, when we work

ALL CHRISTIAN PARENTS ARE INVOLVED IN THE DISCIPLESHIP OF THEIR CHILDREN EVEN IF THEY DON'T KNOW IT

on discipleship from the perspective of the church, we need to nurture a positive relationship with parents as well.

The role of each one could vary over time, in this way:

6–9	10–13	14–17	18–25

6–9

- Children are discipled by their parents.
- Parents are the clearest role model.
- Leaders support parents' leadership.
- Their contact with preteens is vital.

10–13

- Parents are important role models, as are leaders and teachers.
- Parents should get other adults to support their work.
- Their contact with positive teens is vital.

14–17

- Parents model.
- Leaders are mentors.
- Parents should relate with their children's friends.
- Contact with young adults who are good role models is vital.

18–25

- Parents and leaders delegate autonomy.
- Leaders must be life mentors and coaches for specific decisions.
- Contact with young married couples with good relationships is vital.

PARADIGM SHIFTS

- The role of parents changes as the ages advance.
- Leaders without the parents can't get very far.

- The parents must learn to lean on leaders.

IMPLEMENT IDEAS THAT CHANGE THE CULTURE

- Set a good pace for parent meetings based on the age of your students.

- Promote parent-child meetings more often. The interaction that this produces rescues God's design for the church.

- As a disciple, you must always think of each disciple within a family context. There will always be people close to you who can be a good influence on the development of the one you are discipling.

- Let non-Christian parents know that the church is there to help them in their parenthood.

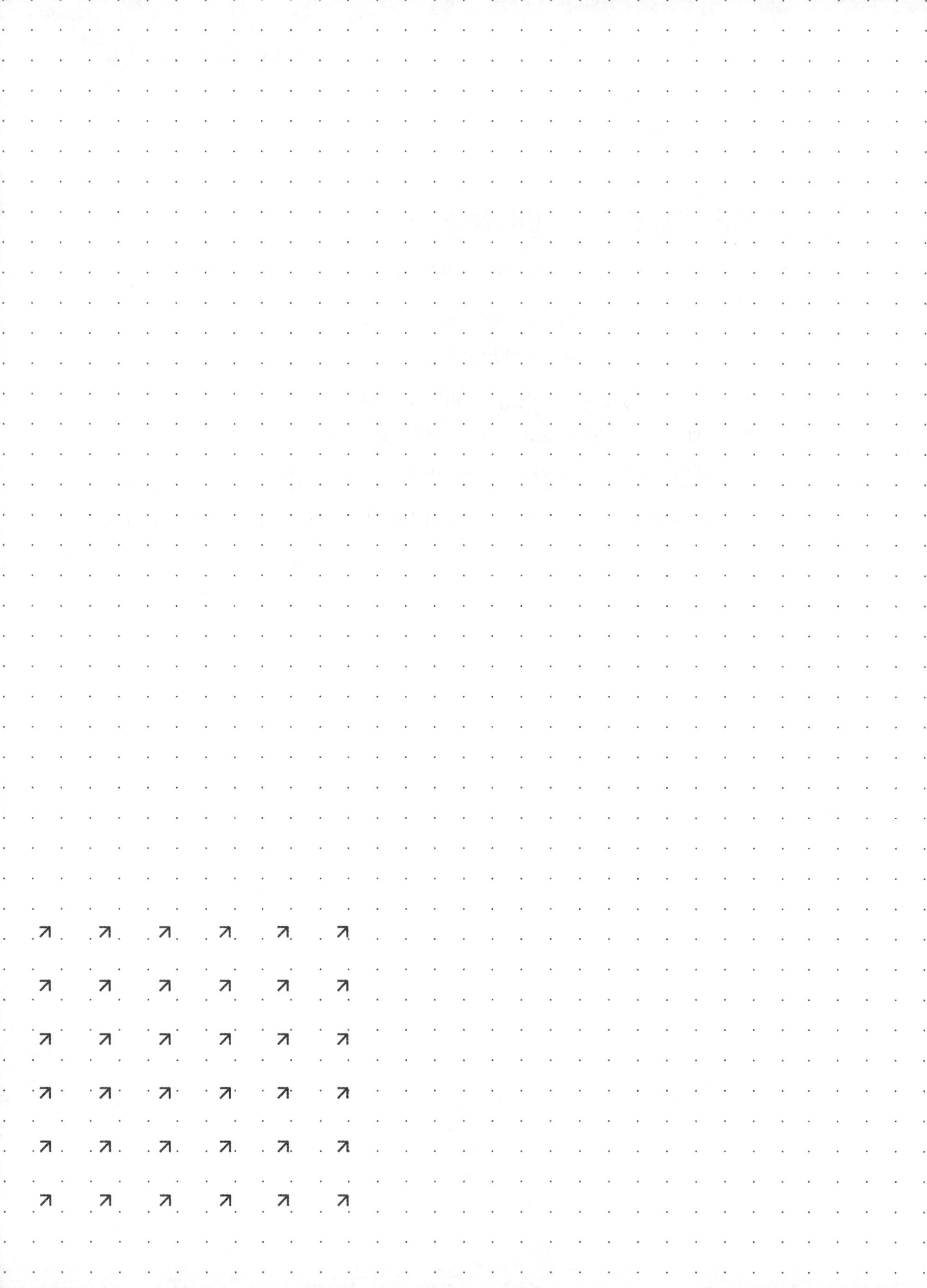

PRINCIPLE 8

THE MIRROR PRINCIPLE

Discipleship is the process of becoming who Jesus would be if He were you.

Dallas Willard

The apostle John made this principle clear: "Whoever claims to live in him must live as Jesus did" (1 John 2:6).

The first great commitment of those of us who dedicate ourselves to the discipleship project is to reflect Christ in everything: his character, passion, decisions, will, and transparency. That is why it is said that no one can disciple if they are not a disciple first. Anyone who is willing to be a disciple tries to look more like Jesus every day since he came, in turn, to reflect the Father. As Paul says, Christ is the image of the invisible God (Colossians 1:15).

The second great commitment is to extend this for others to also resemble Jesus. For this reason we have an exciting and enormous responsibility that can sometimes intimidate us, for which we must also learn from Jesus's dependence on God. In John 15:15 we find him saying: "I no longer call you servants, because a servant does not know his master's business. Instead, I have called you friends, for everything that I learned from my Father I have made known to you."

How good to know that we have a great and powerful God and that he continually renews his mercy for us because we will need it in this process. If we depend on him in the discipleship project, we will surely succeed!

If you think about it, you will see that creation has that same design. Everything that God created has his stamp of ownership. Everything resembles him. Everything was made by him, through him, and for him. Genesis tells the story of the creation of the human being, saying that they were made "in the image and likeness of God" That is, they were created as a mirror that reflects him and starting from this principle, we could design a discipleship process as follows:

1. I know one aspect of the character of Christ. For example: love.

2. I long to be like him in that way.

3. I stop loving my way, to start loving as he loved.

4. I battle against the arguments that prevent me from loving as he loved.

5. I live and practice his love.

6. I teach others to love like him.

7. I choose another aspect of Christ's character to imitate. And so the whole process begins again.

In this way, the discipleship process will last a lifetime, because in each aspect we can find a new depth in the next stage. It is good to be able to work on it with those we have been put in charge of.

PARADIGM SHIFTS

- Reflecting Jesus in our own lives is more important than giving a good sermon or class about Jesus. That means dying to myself so that he can live in me.

- All creation was made in the image of God, and we must and can recover that design.

- Reflecting Christ is not a feeling or a romantic lyric to a cute song but a concrete action in which you model his character.

IMPLEMENT IDEAS THAT CHANGE THE CULTURE

- Choose specific aspects of Jesus's character to reflect on, understand, and develop.

- Prepare a progressive and ordered teaching plan. Put up signs that say something like: "This is the month of love." You can use videos and images for this purpose, and testimonies can be given about experiences of giving and receiving love, so that everyone involved in the discipleship project is clear about the tangible objective that is being worked on.

REFLECTING CHRIST IS NOT A FEELING OR A ROMANTIC LYRIC TO A CUTE SONG BUT A CONCRETE ACTION IN WHICH YOU MODEL HIS CHARACTER.

ACTIVITIES WITH A PURPOSE

Renewing ourselves is not a luxury, it is a necessity for every follower of Jesus in order to continue being agents of restoration and reconciliation in a broken world.

Félix Ortiz

When we mentally leave behind the sanctuary, the classroom, and the liturgy, our panorama expands to the point that we find new scenarios and possibilities to achieve the great purpose of discipleship, which is that the people we influence become more like Jesus.

For the best disciplers, everything is done with a purpose, both relationships and spontaneous conversations at every available opportunity, as well as good programs that facilitate the internalization of desired behaviors.

Some of these activities will be personal or relationship building for a small group. Others, however, should include the community. This is how we teach kids, pre-teens, teens, and young adults to be one body. There character problems will also be revealed, and they will learn to support each other. Then, the disciples will be aware of the reactions of the disciplers to continue forming Christ in them, and the disciplers will also keep an eye as the disciples to imitate them. In those situations, you will realize that they look at you more than you realize.

Remember that it is not about creative ideas just to be creative, or spectacular activities with the desire to be spectacular. From the point of view of the disciple, even the spectacle of a program is simply a pedagogical tool (and not for you

LET US ASK GOD FOR WISDOM TO ENSURE THAT EACH ACTIVITY ALIGNS WITH HIS INTENTIONS FOR OUR MINISTRIES.

to show off). The basic objectives are to promote coexistence, create interest, and facilitate practical lessons in which to model principles.

Think of all these activities from the perspectives of the purpose of discipleship and you will find a new dimension to them:

- Going for a walk outside

- Playing sports

- Climbing a mountain

- Going swimming

- Planting or caring for a tree or plant

- Reading a book

- Visiting the sick, elderly, or orphans

- Watching a movie

- Going to the theater, circus, dance, etc.

- Carrying out a carpentry project

- Playing or singing a song that you can discuss together

- Visiting a relative

The possibilities are endless.

Let us ask God for wisdom to ensure that each activity aligns with his intentions for our ministries.

PARADIGM SHIFTS

- Exercise, play, and fellowship are excellent ministry tools when done with a purpose.

- The activities planned outside the sanctuary are as rich and necessary as those that take place inside.

- Discipleship is not reduced to listening, but disciples must see and act. That is why it is necessary to create these moments with our programs.

IMPLEMENT IDEAS THAT CHANGE THE CULTURE

- Plan for the long term and share the plan with everyone you can.

- Present a public report of all the activities you facilitate outside the sanctuary. It is always better when everyone finds out about the riches that are achieved in personal discipleship.

- Insistently convey to everyone involved in your ministry the idea that your mission is not for them to listen to a biblical proposition quietly and just say amen. It promotes a culture of coexistence, actions, and experiences and not only of sermons and classes.

THE CALL IS FOR EVERYONE

Discipleship is not a choice.
Tim Keller

To think that only pastors have the call to disciple others is nonsense. The great commission to go and make disciples (Matthew 28:16-20; Mark 16:14-18; Luke 24:36-49; John 20:19-23) was given to all the disciples.

If we acknowledge Jesus as our Lord and Savior, then we have a call to discipleship.

All Christians must disciple and doing so is one of the most tremendous ways we can grow because we all learn by teaching. We have all received something that we can give and have learned something that we can teach. Along the way, some are filled with fear or justifications, thinking that they must prepare a lot or that they could make a mistake. But the reality is that we are all in the process of learning because we never stop being disciples, and of course we are going to make mistakes. That is neither something new, nor is it a tragedy.

If Christ trusts us for this task, it must be because we can do it.

If the church continues to believe that one sermon is enough to make disciples, then we will continue to see burnt-out pastors and continue to turn good preachers into celebrities because they speak well, even if they don't help us achieve what God wants us to achieve. God wants disciples and not people with good

IF WE ACKNOWLEDGE JESUS AS OUR LORD AND SAVIOR, THEN WE HAVE A CALL TO DISCIPLESHIP.

morals and some biblical knowledge to behave like Christians in the temple on the weekend.

Disciples.

The sermons, the songs, and the temple are tools and not objectives and when they are used well, they help us to produce disciples of Jesus. And the great news is that there are other tools and mechanisms modeled by Jesus himself to achieve it.

This is where the most important action of all appears: being a model. Modeling is something that adults and even young adults always do for the new generations even if we are not aware that we are doing it. The entire proposal of Generational Leadership is linked to this reality and invites us to be intentional with it. All Christian adults are involved in the discipleship of the youth although perhaps without knowing it. The young adults are ready to disciple the teens because they are already modeling for them what the next stage is all about and the teens, in turn, are doing the same with the preteens and the preteens are being watched by the kids. Modeling is a natural process, and it is much more effective when we are aware of it and do it with devotion, wit, and fidelity.

PARADIGM SHIFTS

- Discipleship is the task of all God's children.

- Pastors and leaders who do not move everyone to disciple sooner or later will burn out or become superficial, or both.

- Discipleship is something that we may already be doing without realizing it, but that we can improve exponentially if we start doing it intentionally.

IMPLEMENT IDEAS THAT CHANGE THE CULTURE

- The importance of discipleship must be communicated privately, publicly, and continually.

- Delegate authority and don't just focus on your work team and volunteers.

- Celebrate what God celebrates and not what the world already celebrates (such as fame, recognition, beauty, or eloquence).

- Involve new generations in ministry and discipleship at an early age. They are already looking at us.

10 LESSONS FOR DISCIPLING TEENS

Discipleship is a call to an exciting adventure, and it is also a huge challenge.

The teenage stage is characterized by the enormous amount of emotions, ideas, thoughts, and choices that arise in the development of identity. When we work in the discipleship of teenagers, we are building the foundations of character and personality that will govern their lives in the future. For this reason, each lesson that we carry out, each meeting, and each individual space for mentoring and accompaniment must be an intentional moment to affirm their identity in Christ and their character on that rock. In addition, we must manage to give the disciples all the necessary tools so that they never get stuck in religious inertia.

The following lessons are designed under the sequence or model AFFIRM which uses the process developed in the following acrostic:

 **A**valanche of ideas

 **F**oundations of the theme

 **F**ocus on truth

 **I**ntrospection

 **R**eflect on a character

Mobilize

This "AFFIRM" model facilitates a discipleship process in which both teachers and each learner are challenged to grow and mature.

These are details for each stage:

1. **Avalanche of ideas.** It collects diverse opinions about the proposed topic: what is heard among teens, what is said in the streets, and what society perceives from different points of view.

2. **Foundations of the theme.** It is a compendium of theoretical foundations that help us clarify ideas and generate biblical, scientific, and philosophical support on the proposed topic.

3. **Focus on truth.** Contains the necessary biblical development to form the teenager in the principles of the Word of God. The expressed criteria point to teenagers being able to find the answers to the problems of life in Scripture.

4. **Introspection.** It includes questions that help the teen to acquire an adequate criterion on the subject based on their own analysis. You can include open discussions to hear the opinions of other members of the group.

5. **Reflect on a character.** In this section we are committed to talking about two characters. The first will be a current character, known and admired among teens, and the second will be a biblical character.

6. **Mobilize.** Here discipler and disciple generate together a list of specific actions to be implemented after finishing the lesson. In this way, the topic does not remain theoretical, but encourages the teen to put what they have learned into practice.

This sequence will also help you create other topics and lessons or enhance other materials that you can access on www.e625.com.

The one who leads the discipleship (you!) must study the lesson and delve into it to later determine the treatment they want to give at each step. Some topics will be hotter and more urgent, depending on the disciples' context, so some lessons could last one, two, or three weeks, depending on what you, your team, and the Holy Spirit dictate.

That's right.

It will be essential for each discipler to walk in a close relationship with the Holy Spirit so that they can be guided by him and thus impact a new generation of disciples.

WARNING:

From here we assume that you have already carefully read about the essential principles of biblical discipleship in Section 1, and that all members of your team have gone through prior tactical training to carry out the lessons that begin below.

We already made it clear that parents are the first to be called to disciple their children, so it's not a bad idea for you to start this material with a mini training for them as well, or at least with a presentation informing them that you will be sharing the following lessons from this discipleship project with your children.

This project tries to mobilize more people to take up the challenge of not continuing to sit in religious comfort, but to help the generations that come next, inside and outside the meetings or sanctuaries.

THE ROLLER COASTER OF EMOTIONS

The pathway to unleashing the transformative power of Jesus to heal our spiritual lives can be found in the joining of emotional health and contemplative spirituality.

Peter Scazzero, *Emotionally Healthy Spirituality*

The drivers are bursting with adrenaline every time they start the engines of their convertibles. Loud music, muscular guys, hot girls, and the exciting betting on illegal street races. Speed, adventure, competition, and in the middle of it all, love stories that are woven into the plot of the chase scenes. The combination of all these factors is what gave the classic *Fast and Furious* saga great success. In the first installments, the production was simple and with unknown actors, but the mix of so many youthful emotions ensured these films a fast and furious success.

This is how teenagers want to live life, right? And if not, at least it seems that they do, because without the production, stunts, or explosions; some of them experience the same emotions of a movie.

In this type of film, the key is to make viewers identify with the protagonists, to feel brave and capable of performing the most incredible feats, and there comes a point where everything crosses the line into reality.

Impressive falls, jumps between buildings, cars floating on parachutes, miraculous feats; and we are left gawking, even though our minds know that all of this is impossible. Why does it attract us even though it's so fantastic? Because it connects with our desires. It is important that you know that your teens may not want to skydive, but they do want to live exciting lives, be attractive, and do something meaningful. To do that they must learn to work on their emotions.

Start your discipleship group by referring to these movies, or others your teens like, and ask them what makes those movies so exciting and why they appeal to so many people. Ask them how they make other fans (and not themselves) feel, and they'll throw in some wild theories, too.

Of course, another option is to play a game or activity that allows them to experience different emotions (there are several at www.e625.com) or start the lesson in an amusement park with roller coasters and other games that fascinate teenagers. The idea is to trigger the topic of emotions to help them get into the conversation.

AVALANCHE OF IDEAS

Mood swings are a classic feature of the teenage years. You can study about this in different psychology research papers. However, to get to know teens, the most powerful resource you have is the teens themselves. Present different hypothetical situations and ask them to tell you what they would feel in each of them.

HERE ARE SOME SUGGESTIONS

- Driving a racecar

- Winning an Oscar or Grammy

- Catching the eye of the models walking down a catwalk

- Going skydiving

- When your team wins the international championship

- When the person you like makes eye contact with you

- When something embarrassing happens to you

- The divorce of your parents

- When someone betrays your trust

- The death of a person you cared about

The question is always, "How would this make you feel?" Depending on your group, you can even challenge them to act out these situations in pairs (and you'll be surprised how many good actors and actresses you have).

Note that the examples, although they do not follow a strict order, go from joy to sadness. Take time to explore each idea until the group can feel some emotion. Try to get them to imagine the situation by closing their eyes or acting out the situations.

At the end, and if it did not already arise naturally, you can ask two of them to talk about a a time in their lives when they experienced a very strong emotion. It is common for boys and girls of this age to experience emotions very intensely in the different situations that they go through, and the idea of discipleship is for teenagers to feel accompanied by someone more mature while they go through this phase of life.

📝 FOUNDATIONS OF THE THEME

Now it's necessary to teach your group a little about feelings and emotions. The difference between these two words is explained as follows:

Emotions are intense and short-lived. They carry a large dose of hormones and, just as they appear suddenly, they disappear in the same way. Some examples of emotions are anger, joy, rage, or passion.

Feelings take longer to appear, they arise little by little, and the experience is maintained for a longer time. For example: the illusion of falling in love, sadness, mild anger, or frustration. In any case, some feelings can become very intense and stay that way for a long time, while some can even turn into pathologies such as depression.

TEENAGERS NEED TO EXPERIENCE UNCONDITIONAL LOVE.

It's important that your teenagers know that the stage they are living is a season of many emotional ups and downs, and that this is normal. Although it may be difficult for them to bear, if they know more about the subject they will be able to handle it in a better way. Mood swings during the teen years are frequent, unexpected, and for no apparent reason. We, as disciplers, must be attentive to them while we accompany our boys and girls at this stage.

Something we should not forget is that we must also be connected with their parents. Teenagers often experience situations in which they need those they love the most to be willing to listen and love them unconditionally. Parents must be trained in this, and warned about the emotional changes that their children are experiencing or will experience.

📖 FOCUS ON TRUTH

There are some emotions that are positive, while others can be dangerous if we let them fester. The Word of God contains some advice on this, as it does for all aspects of life, advice that can help us to better understand and manage our emotions. Let's look at, for example, Proverbs 15. (You can read the whole chapter if you want to go deeper with your group, but we'll just look at a few verses here.)

"A gentle answer turns away wrath, but a harsh word stirs up anger." (v.1)

"A happy heart makes the face cheerful, but heartache crushes the spirit." (v.13)

"All the days of the oppressed are wretched, but the cheerful heart has a continual feast." (v.15)

"A hot-tempered person stirs up conflict, but the one who is patient calms a quarrel." (v.18)

As you can see, the book of Proverbs contains a lot of wisdom! Here we chose these four verses as examples of emotions and how to handle them:

- Verse 1 tells us about anger. We can all get angry, but there is a real and 100% effective alternative to calm another person's anger, and that is to respond kindly.

- Verse 13 tells us about joy and a happy heart. Joy can change a person's face. But there is also the antithesis, sadness, which can provoke a person's spirit to become troubled.

- Verse 15 speaks of afflictions and sadness. There is not a single person in the world who does not feel sadness, and it is good to feel it when there are legitimate causes such as the death of a loved one. But we must learn to channel it positively, and never lose the joy that gratitude produces.

- Verse 18 talks about anger again and how it relates to fighting. But it also presents us with a hopeful fact: anger can be controlled!

Now let's look at a text in which Paul speaks to the believers in the Corinthian church about sadness:

"Godly sorrow brings repentance that leads to salvation and leaves no regret, but worldly sorrow brings death."
2 Corinthians 7:10

Here the apostle Paul is making a play on words and establishing a contrast. There are two types of sadness. The one that has to do with guilt, which is dissipated with repentance, and on the other hand, the sadness of the world, which has to do with the anxiety that society transmits and that does not produce anything good in us.

When we sin, the Holy Spirit speaks to our conscience, and it fills us with sadness with the aim of leaving the sin and getting closer to God (which, for Paul and for the Bible in general, is synonymous with life). On the contrary, the sadness that the world produces is usually an anxiety for not feeling loved enough, and that comes by and kills our hearts.

So, let's also talk about love!

The Word of God says many things about love, but something that is extremely important is knowing how to distinguish between spiritual love and sentimental or romantic love. They are two different things.

Romantic love is a human feeling that brings you closer to a person with the intention of establishing a relationship, although we also emotionally love close people with whom we have experienced important things. In the stage of adolescence, with the accumulation of emotions and feelings mixed in, triggering unpredictable attitudes and behaviors, it is necessary for boys and girls to realize that it is not a stage in which love of this nature can be handled wisely. The mistake of many teenagers is to think that they can handle it.

But let's also talk about spiritual love, or *agape* love. This is a different love, which is not limited to human emotions, but transcends to eternity. This kind of love helps us make mature and conscious decisions.

> *"My command is this: Love each other as I have loved you. Greater love has no one than this: to lay down one's life for one's friends. You are my friends if you do what I command."*
> **John 15:12–14**

What a powerful passage! It tells us that love, as a human feeling, has its limitations, but the love we learn from God is wild! No kind of human love is greater than that of someone who gives their life for someone else. On the other hand, verse 14 tells us that we will be considered friends of God (in agape love), if we do what he commands us, that is, if we are obedient.

It's interesting to note that for human beings love is usually measured based on what we feel, while genuine and spiritual love is measured based on how obedient we are to God's instructions. We can also see that when there is no agape love in people's lives, they get carried away by erotic, passionate, sentimental, human, and limited love.

Which kind of love would you like to be loved with?

Emotions compete within us to get out, and we can feed the best of them.

 INTROSPECTION

Prepare some simple posters, one for each emotion, or write them on a board, or send them pictures online if your meeting is virtual. (You can also include the definitions of each on the posters.) About six posters would be fine. Then ask the group to each tell a personal story with the emotion they choose, to discard the word. You can break the ice by telling your own story.

Perhaps you can do it with some of the most difficult emotions, such as grudges. This is voluntary, and everyone can share what they want, but you as a discipler must be attentive to the emotions that each boy or girl shows while telling their story. Indicate to them how much time each one has to speak, and that they discard the emotion words as they go through them, this will help you to set a better pace and a goal to the activity.

The main purpose here is not to generate laughter or tears in the group, but to make them a little more vulnerable as they open their hearts to tell something personal, and that they may discover that others have had similar experiences. These kinds of activities are always best done in small groups, which is great because that's what discipleship is all about.

 # REFLECT ON A CHARACTER

BILLIE EILISH

The 2020 Grammy Awards awarded four prizes to Billie Eilish in recognition of her songs. Despite being barely 18 years old, this revelation demonstrated her ability to rub shoulders with the greats of music. Millions of teenagers love her songs and others hate them, but, for one reason or another, she was on everyone's lips.

At the age of 14, she achieved fame with her first single *Ocean Eyes* and far from what one might assume, this success was not enough to help her get out of her constant battles with depression. Billie has received treatment to manage this type of emotion, without victory yet (as she has stated in her interviews). Anyone might think that being successful and having lots of money should help her lead an emotionally stable life, but it doesn't. On the contrary, just like for many others who live in the artistic field, success has become its own prison.

QUESTIONS FOR THE DISCIPLES

- What is missing for Billie Eilish to know?

- What do you tend to feel when you hear her music?

- What type of lessons can we learn from Billie's story? Why?

Lead your disciples to share some insights about depression and other similar feelings that plague them. Surely some of them have dealt with or are dealing with some form of depression, and the fact that they manage to talk about it will be the beginning to help work through it.

SAUL

The first king of Israel was named Saul and we find his story in the first book of Samuel, beginning with chapter nine. Biblical history says that Saul was anointed to be king by the prophet Samuel, that he was a very tall and handsome man, and that he was honored and respected by all of God's people. He won many battles and was a good king in the first years of his reign, but there was something he couldn't shake: Saul did not think he was capable of doing what God had called him to do. He felt inferior, and that feeling led him to make several mistakes.

Although he initially had a good heart, his soul gradually changed and he began to disobey certain specific commands from God, which ultimately ended his reign. Saul was wrong to such an extent that, on one occasion, the prophet Samuel himself had to go and correct him, telling him that it was better to obey God than to sacrifice many sheep. This was said because Saul thought that making many sacrifices would make up for his disobedience.

CONTROLLING EMOTIONS IN ADOLESCENCE CAN SEEM LIKE A MASSIVE CHALLENGE, BUT IT'S NOT IMPOSSIBLE.

In the last stages of his reign, Saul already felt afflicted, overwhelmed by the condition of his soul, and at a certain moment he met David, a shepherd who, with the playing of his harp, managed to calm that feeling of anguish that followed Saul. However, that didn't last too long either. After David defeated the giant Goliath, Saul began to develop a lot of jealousy and envy against this young warrior who had won the favor of the people. Everyone cheered for David, and Saul felt jealous and distrustful. Thus, little by little Saul lost confidence in David, and his emotions led him to persecute David who, by then, had already been anointed as the new king of Israel.

Saul did not have a good ending, and in large part it was because he did not know how to handle his emotions properly.

QUESTIONS FOR THE DISCIPLES

- What do you do when you feel jealous of someone?

- How do you manage this and other negative emotions?

MOBILIZE

Controlling emotions in adolescence may seem like a massive challenge, but it's not impossible. One of the keys to this is knowing the goodness of the Spirit of God in us. When you look at the list of manifestations of the fruit of the Spirit in the book of Galatians, you will see that they have a lot to do with a development in the spiritual dimension of each person, which helps them to manage emotions properly.

But the fruit of the Spirit is love, joy, peace, forbearance, kindness, goodness, faithfulness, gentleness and self-control. Against such things there is no law.
Galatians 5:22–23

Try the exercise of writing a list of the manifestations of the fruit of the Spirit of God (there are 9) and, at the same time, identify the possible emotions that are related to them.

MANIFESTATIONS OF THE FRUIT OF THE SPIRIT OF GOD	RELATED HUMAN EMOTIONS AND FEELINGS (SOME ARE POSITIVE, OTHERS NEGATIVE)
Love	Illusion, tenderness, passion, friendship, hate, …
Joy	Joy, jubilation, euphoria, sadness, nostalgia, melancholy, …
Peace	Worry, affliction, tranquility, restlessness, …
Patience	Impatience, frustration, despair, apathy, …
Kindness	Rage, anger, interest, envy, compassion, …

Goodness	Malice, machinations, indolence, jealousy, compassion,...
Faithfulness	Betrayal, trust, distrust, hope, fear, ...
Gentleness	Pride, resentment, discouragement, ...
Self-Control	Shame, guilt, tension, tolerance, ...

The list of emotions and feelings that could be included in each row of this table is endless, but one thing is clear: the manifestations of the fruit of the Spirit of God have their counterpart in the emotions and feelings that we experience. Therefore, manifesting all the attributes of that fruit is not achieved in a week, nor in a month. This requires a lifetime.

With this in mind, how about we make a plan for the future? A commitment before God where each disciple can, first, identify those emotions that they usually cannot handle. Then, in response to that inability, they must find that dimension of the fruit of the Spirit with which it relates and ask Christ to begin to transform that area of their life. What you can do is guide them toward it with some questions:

- Which, of the many that exist, are the emotions that dominate you?

- Who or what things do you usually react badly to?

- Which of the nine manifestations of the fruit of the Spirit of God do you think is the one you need the most?

- What actions do you think you could take to make this dimension of the fruit of the Spirit come true in your life?

LESSON 2

IDENTITY AND SELF-ESTEEM

Immature people spend more energy looking good than being better.

Lucas Leys, *Stamina*

You may be familiar with the movie *The Truman Show*, but your teens may not be. In the movie, everything happens on a TV set, but the protagonist doesn't know that, and believes everything is real. Truman Burbank was born and raised among a collusion of actors and extras, all trained by the director of a reality television show to broadcast to the world, through the screen, a person's life in real time.

The core of the movie *The Truman Show* lies precisely in the suspicion and search of Truman, who begins to notice some strange things that happen around him. Truman, played by Jim Carrey, is looking for the truth, he's looking to find out who he is, while everyone around him is concentrating on not letting Truman discover that truth.

Who is this man? Someone who lost his identity because his life was a reality show instead of real life. Everyone in the world knew who Truman was. The only one who didn't know who he was, was Truman himself.

Sadly, the plot of this movie resembles the life of many teenagers.

Use this text describing the movie *The Truman Show*, or some other similar examples, to introduce the topic to your group: in this lesson we will talk about the development of a clear identity with a healthy self-esteem. Start with these questions:

- How would you feel if you suddenly found out that your life has been an entertainment show?

- Who could you trust if you suspected that everyone was lying to you?

AVALANCHE OF IDEAS

A few years ago, it was unusual for teenagers to speak out about identity or self-esteem. Today, the terms are so widespread on the internet that if you ask a teenager for their opinion on identity or self-esteem, they will surely give you a pretty accurate answer. Some of them will even give you a psychological report on their own condition, and they will define themselves as someone with high or low self-esteem. But that does not mean that they are totally clear on the subject.

Despite having so much information at their fingertips with the click of a button, most teens don't know how to heal their sense of worth if it's not in its place, and thus most walk through life without a sense of future nor a defined identity.

Toss them the following statements and ask them to discuss if they think they are true or false, and why. (In this part you only explore what comes to mind when they hear these statements, without sharing your personal opinions.)

- People you admire, such as celebrities, define your identity.

- Teenagers are easily influenced by their friends.

- Identity is achieved when you can look enough like someone else.

- The things that others say about you define your self-esteem.

- Parents can raise or lower their children's self-esteem.

- Healthy self-esteem does not depend on others, but on oneself.

- Someone with low self-esteem is a weak person.

Allow time to respond to each one before moving on to the next.

At the end, also ask them:

- What is self-esteem?

- What is identity?

- What is the relationship between those two concepts?

- Do you think you have a clear identity? Why or why not?

- Do you think you have a healthy self-esteem? Why or why not?

DESPITE HAVING SO MUCH INFORMATION AT THEIR FINGERTIPS, MOST TEENS DON'T KNOW HOW TO HEAL THEIR SENSE OF WORTH IF IT'S NOT IN ITS PLACE.

FOUNDATIONS OF THE THEME

Based on the *"Manual de consejería para el trabajo con adolescentes"* (*Counseling manual for work with adolescents*) by e625, the construction of identity involves three important and very well marked stages: the stage of self-discovery, the stage of formation of the life project, and the stage of the inclusion of the different spheres of life.

Identity can be defined as the process of building a person in terms of their essence, nature, personality, vocation, and, above all, character.

According to the different sciences, although there are some genetic elements that make identity, it is a construction that each individual creates.

The constant sensory recording of moments lived since childhood lays the foundations of what we are going to be in the future. These moments are called milestones. A milestone is that memorable memory that gives us a guideline on how to react at every moment of life.

The teenager will model their behavior based on these milestones and will unconsciously want to obtain what they felt in them. The famously bizarre, irritable, and antisocial behavior of teenagers is part of an ongoing search for "emotional justice." They are trying to complete what they feel is unfinished, and fill what they feel is empty, and their reactions will be based on that search.

THE FAMOUSLY BIZARRE, IRRITABLE, AND ANTISOCIAL BEHAVIOR OF TEENAGERS IS PART OF AN ONGOING SEARCH FOR "EMOTIONAL JUSTICE."

If these conflicts cannot be resolved, a large part of their adult life will become a search to fill those deficiencies of childhood and adolescence. As a discipler, you have a precious opportunity to lay firm foundations for their future. In addition, you will be able to participate in this very special stage in which the foundations of their life projects are laid.

It is now, in adolescence, as part of the construction of their identity and self-esteem, that they will consider the possibilities of the future. And you will be there to help them.

Regarding self-esteem, you will have to fight together with them against various manifestations of today's society that directly affect the self-esteem of teenagers. Some of the enemies of a healthy personal assessment can be bullying, toxic relationships with close people, violence at home, parental divorce, or the hurtful and paralyzing words that teenagers hear daily. The consequences of these enemies of self-esteem can vary: addictions, inappropriate sexual behavior, school dropout, rebellion, depression, etc.

Much of your work in discipling teens will involve bringing these issues up for discussion and helping them process better. Bringing to light what affects those you disciple will be a good first step in giving them the freedom to build a healthier self-esteem, discarding those milestones that have sunk them and highlighting those that are positive.

📖 FOCUS ON TRUTH

Read with them the following verses:

> *When Jesus came to the region of Caesarea Philippi, he asked his disciples, "Who do people say the Son of Man is?"*
>
> *They replied, "Some say John the Baptist; others say Elijah; and still others, Jeremiah or one of the prophets."*
>
> *"But what about you?" he asked. "Who do you say I am?"*
>
> *Simon Peter answered, "You are the Messiah, the Son of the living God."*
>
> *Jesus replied, "Blessed are you, Simon son of Jonah, for this was not revealed to you by flesh and blood, but by my Father in heaven.*
>
> **Matthew 16:13–17**

This portion of Scripture shows Jesus discussing his identity and what people were saying about him. They gave him some options, but Jesus really didn't care what other people said about him, but only what his closest friends said of him. That is why he asked them the same question again:

"Who do you say I am?"

For Peter, this conversation was not only important, it was defining. Peter's affirmation that Jesus was the Messiah, the Son of the living God, the Christ, gave him a powerful "spiritual moment." "God has blessed you," Jesus told him, and he recognized that this revelation did not come from human wisdom, but from God himself. Look how the text continues:

> *And I tell you that you are Peter, and on this rock I will build my church, and the gates of Hades will not overcome it. I will give you the*

keys of the kingdom of heaven; whatever you bind on earth will be bound in heaven, and whatever you loose on earth will be loosed in heaven.

Matthew 16:18-19

So, being clear about the identity of Jesus changed Peter's life forever and reaffirmed the reason why Jesus had changed his name, giving meaning to his spiritual identity. The same can happen with us!

When we clarify the identity of Jesus, we also clarify our own identify.

Furthermore, each of us would do well to repeat this reflective conversation in our own lives. Many times, we pay too much attention to the opinions of people, such as classmates and other circumstantial companions, but we forget that only the closest people are important in this sense. Those with whom we have opened up enough to know the depths of our hearts are the ones who can best comment on our identity. That is why it is vital to choose wisely who these people will be, in addition to those who are part of our family.

Disciplers should be able to access that level with our teenagers! They should listen to what we have to say about them because, thanks to the relationship we are building, we can tell them how we see them for who they really are, despite what the world tells them.

Now let's read this passage of Scripture that teaches us about the relationship between God's love and our identity:

See what great love the Father has lavished on us, that we should be called children of God! And that is what we are! The reason the world does not know us is that it did not know him.

1 John 3:1

Thanks to his infinite love we can call ourselves children of God! Our status as children makes us part of a family of which God is the Father, and therefore he is the one who can best assign us identity.

From this passage we can learn two things:

1. God, who is perfect, is also a perfect Father, and because he loves us as children, then we can be sure that he loves us in a special way.

2. Those who do not know God cannot recognize us as children of God, and will always assign us a wrong identity.

Knowing all this is key to building identity. The greatest challenge for a teenager (and for the whole world) in building their identity is being able to see themselves as God sees them, recognizing the rock on which to build who they are going to become.

Knowing what God thinks of us raises our self-esteem. On the contrary, listening to what the devil says against us makes us lose ourselves in doubt and shame, and makes us feel incapable of being what God says we are.

> **THE GREATEST CHALLENGE FOR A TEENAGER IN BUILDING THEIR IDENTITY IS BEING ABLE TO SEE THEMSELVES AS GOD SEES THEM.**

 # INTROSPECTION

This is the time to help your teens reflect on what is on their hearts with the following questions:

- Who are you listening to? Do you listen to God's truths about your life, which lift you up and propel you toward the fulfillment of your purpose? Or do you listen to the enemy's lies that sink you into a bottomless pit?

- What is necessary to do today to build the future you want?

- What positive things do you have that may enable you, to achieve what you have proposed?

- What attitudes should you change?

- What kind of identity are you building?

- With whom should you get right, ask forgiveness, forgive, etc.?

 REFLECT ON A CHARACTER

SELENA GOMEZ

Selena Gomez became one of the most recognized Disney actresses worldwide. Her support for social aid projects such as A21 (against human trafficking) was reported across many media platforms, and she was seen singing at a special event in a very popular church.

However, we all know that most Disney kids or teens have had various problems coping with their popularity, and she was no exception. Imagine that your life stops being private and becomes public, and that everything you do or say is seen or heard by millions of people of all languages and cultures. That's not easy for anyone!

This happened to Selena, who has stated in many of her interviews that she struggled against depression and anxiety, to the point of having to attend therapy continuously.

Anyone might wonder: how can a highly successful girl, admired by many for her talent and beauty, feel depressed? The answer is very simple, and it is that if our identity and self-esteem are based on fleeting things like beauty, or on things we need to work hard at, then we will never feel that what we do is enough.

This may be a good time to pray for some artists, singers, actors and actresses, and other members of the entertainment world who need to understand what Christ can do if they let him into their lives.

QUESTIONS FOR THE DISCIPLES

- Why do you think so many people admire TV stars or influencers?

- What is their true worth?

- Why is popularity not a reliable source of identity and self-esteem?

JOHN, THE APOSTLE

Here we are talking about the writer of the most intimate Gospel of the Bible, and also the one to whom the book of Revelation was given. But it is not only those books of the Bible that allow us to know this apostle in depth but, above all, his pastoral letters.

John wrote in a very intimate way. His Gospel is called "the gospel of love" surely because the author's intention was to make known to the world the supernatural love that he had experienced while being close to Jesus. On the other hand, some see the messages to the churches narrated in the first chapters of the book of Revelation as rigid warnings from a God who brings justice. However, when reading John's writings, we see that he did not speak tragically, but rather about God's protection and deep concern for human beings.

When John begins his letters, he speaks to his disciples calling them "little children." Such endearing affection is not only a personality quality, but clear evidence of having received that same affection from the eternal Father. John considers the fact of being called children by God as a great sign of love. John was sure of who he was in Christ, and knowing God deeply through Jesus allowed him to speak as he did.

QUESTIONS FOR THE DISCIPLES

- Could you say similar things to what John said? Why or why not?

- In what ways is John worthy of imitation?

🖐 MOBILIZE

A large part of the work of a discipler consists of getting involved in the lives of those whom they are discipling, contacting their family, and creating some casual encounters and other intentional spaces where they can go deeper in the process of accompaniment.

Remember that it is very possible that any specific action you take in this process will become a milestone: an enduring memory that will serve as a reference in the life of that boy or girl. They will remember it forever, and many of their future actions will be influenced by that memory.

What milestones can you create in your relationship with your disciples?

HERE ARE SOME IDEAS

- **Public recognition.** Create a space within services or adolescent meetings to recognize the positive qualities that each boy or girl has. Highlight their successes, their talents, thank them for their good deeds, and give them the impetus to keep going. If you focus on one or two of them each week, throughout the year you can reach all your teenagers.

- **Self-esteem meeting.** Organize a meeting for teens to say positive things to each other, mainly about the future. It will be better if you do it in a small group. Set everyone the task of imagining what every other boy and girl will be like in 5 or 10 years. Warn them not to see negative things but positive ones: professional successes, use of their talents, healthy personal relationships, etc.

- **Visit their home.** You can schedule a visit to talk with their parents and tell them all the positive things you see in their child. Focus on the talents and abilities that you see in them. Be on the lookout if either parent tries to use this time to complain about their son's or daughter's behavior. You must be very skillful and wise to turn the complaint into a possibility of positive change for the future.

Remember that this material is not designed to be rushed to complete a curriculum, but you can extend it as much as you want. You could use a week for each topic, or up to a month if you wanted. From one lesson you may want to branch out to several sessions, using different activities and topics to complete a deeper process in the development of those who are under your care.

INTERNAL EXPLOSIONS

Humility was the beauty of Christ's character and his approach. It was also an oasis where his leadership was refreshed.

Lucas Leys, *The Greatest Leader of All Time*

Which movie character is most famous for his outbursts of anger?

The answer is almost unequivocal.

Of course, it's the Hulk!

The Hulk was a scientist who, while doing experiments with gamma rays, ended up having his genetics affected forever. We all know the result: Bruce Banner can live his life calmly and normally, but only until someone angers him. What happens then? An internal explosion. Every cell in his body begins to change, turning him into a monstrous green figure.

Do you know people like that? Surely you do! And it's not pretty, is it? However, this can happen to all of us if we don't get anger under control early.

🧠 AVALANCHE OF IDEAS

In Lesson 1 we mentioned some aspects of emotions, but now we will talk about character, clarifying that, although they are related, they are not the same thing.

Ask your teens to complete the following survey (and you can do it too!). In this list of "character defects," each one should choose a number from 1 to 5 to represent their personal situation (1 if it is something that does not control them at all; 5 if they recognize that it is a major defect in their life). In this way they will be able to evaluate which are the most urgent aspects they must work on.

Envy _______	Authoritarianism _______	Starting things I don't end up finishing _______
Desire for revenge _______	Irritability _______	Not recognizing my own mistakes _______
Selfishness _______	Laziness _______	Arrogance _______
Pride _______	Jealousy _______	Tendency to lie _______
Vanity _______	Apathy _______	Self-justification _______
Resentment _______	Aggression _______	Emotional instability _______
Headstrong _______	Being in a bad mood _______	Constant criticism _______
Irrational fears _______	Possessiveness _______	Dependency on others _______

Sometimes it's hard to be objective when evaluating ourselves, right? A second option is that you can give your teenagers this list of "character defects" and ask those people to find some people who know them well and ask them to fill out the same survey. Parents and siblings may be good candidates, but it will also work with their closest friends. Even you, as a discipler, could also make an evaluation of each one of the teens you are discipling, although it is necessary that you emphasize that the important thing is not to just put a score but to evaluate in order to help and love them better.

At the end of this process, they will collect the data and compare it. It may come as a surprise for many to observe the differences between their own evaluation and those of others. And it will be very interesting for each one to know the way in which others see them, especially if they are people they live with or are close to (although you may want to consider making the surveys "anonymous" so that no one can feel hurt by a particular person's comments). A good idea to anticipate the concrete actions at the end of the lesson is to plan with each disciple a process of personal development of those areas of their character that, according to the survey, they have recognized need attention. The idea is not that you help them do everything, but that each disciple can take personal steps to change those aspects of their life and character that they recognize need to change. Remind them that mature character development is a critical key to their future lives, which will affect their calling, family, work, and ministry.

THE MATURE CHARACTER DEVELOPMENT IS A CRITICAL KEY TO THEIR FUTURE LIVES

 # FOUNDATIONS OF THE THEME

Alex Sampedro writes in his book *Artesano* [*Craftsman*]: "True transformation happens little by little. With small changes that end up becoming collective habits. With small seeds that, with patience and time, occupy a field. In more humble but lasting ways. They are not that spectacular, but they are real."

One of the things that all disciples must clearly understand is that times of trials and difficulties come in order to form our character. Each test passed will be one more step toward maturity, but failing a test will mean that it will come back for you to go through it again. This does not have to do with a relentless God who wants our harm, but with the enormous desire of the Father to form his children as he imagined them to be: strengthened in him and capable of living according to his will. That requires building character.

Character defects that are not overcome are a sign of a person's inability to mature. Someone who is immature can destroy their most important relationships, squander their career opportunities, and faint when they most need to be on their feet. Due to immaturity, loved ones are hurt, marriages and families are destroyed, and envy or greed can be harbored in the heart. And because of immaturity, many can fall into addictions from which it will be difficult for them to get out.

ALL DISCIPLES MUST CLEARLY UNDERSTAND THAT TRIALS AND DIFFICULTIES COME IN ORDER TO FORM OUR CHARACTER.

Therefore, developing the character of Christ is a great challenge for every disciple.

What, then, are the things that lay the groundwork for building a strong character?

- **A life of constant communication with God.** While it's true that we all have different ways of connecting with God, we need to make sure that we have constant access to his presence, and we need to make that connection regularly.

- **Spiritual disciplines.** Worship, prayer, fasting, reading and studying the Word of God, meditation and memorization of his Word; all are good disciplines that a disciple must develop to form a strong character.

- **Accountability.** Having someone to whom we can voluntarily give an account of our life, promotes a strength in our inner being that is difficult to replicate. When we are vulnerable to someone else, we become people of increasingly strong character. This also makes us humbler and prevents us from stumbling.

- **Firm convictions.** The fact of not letting ourselves be blown away by the winds of information means that we are not like the waves of the sea, as the letter of James says.

- **Self-control.** Emotional reactions arise from an immature character and need to be controlled. It is not that emotions are wrong, but that we cannot allow ourselves to be governed by them.

📖 FOCUS ON TRUTH

Read with them the following verses:

As you come to him, the living Stone rejected by humans but chosen by God and precious to him you also, like living stones, are being built into a spiritual house to be a holy priesthood, offering spiritual sacrifices acceptable to God through Jesus Christ.

1 Peter 2:4–5

Here the apostle Peter tells us about Christ as the living Stone, a strong and firm foundation on which we build our lives. The material of this foundation is heavenly, eternal, and precious. It refers to the attributes and character of Christ. In the same way, Peter speaks to the church, and consequently to each one of us, assuring us that we are living stones just like Jesus, since the Father builds us with the same heavenly, eternal, and precious material as Christ. This speaks of what we are in essence: a spiritual house.

Also, a stone is part of an altar. Therefore, we are also the lit altar of living stones on which sacrifices of worship to the Father are performed. As long as the foundation is laid in Jesus, the living stone, the eternal rock, we will be building this spiritual house well.

Our condition and growth are so important in the construction process of the church that if a stone does not fulfill its proper function, the entire building is at risk. Christ is the example, and for this reason he is the foundation. In him there is no deceit or shadow of doubt. Jesus fulfilled all the law and was perfect in everything.

To this you were called, because Christ suffered for you, leaving you an example, that you should follow in his steps. "He committed no sin, and no deceit was found in his mouth."

1 Peter 2:21–22

Following in the footsteps of Christ means turning your back on sin. To be molded according to the character of Christ is to cross the desert of doubt and not stop believing; suffer judgment and shame, and respond meekly; suffer injustice and act with self-control; to be rejected, hurt, betrayed, and despite all this have a forgiving spirit. All these actions define a mature character.

When they hurled their insults at him, he did not retaliate; when he suffered, he made no threats. Instead, he entrusted himself to him who judges justly. "He himself bore our sins" in his body on the cross, so that we might die to sins and live for righteousness; "by his wounds you have been healed."

1 Peter 2:23-24

Questions to reflect on:

- How do you respond when you are insulted?

- What is your reaction when an injustice is committed against you?

- What do you do when someone lies to you?

- How do you act when someone makes you suffer?

- What feelings does your heart have against the people who have hurt you?

IF YOUR HEART HAS AREAS THAT ARE NOT GOVERNED BY JESUS, THESE AREAS WILL BE IMMATURE AND WILL BE CARRIED AWAY BY THE DESIRES OF THE FLESH.

Each of these questions can help us to assess our degree of maturity. It's not just about putting your head down and letting the whole world finish you off. On the contrary, the ideal would be to be so aligned with the voice of the Spirit of God that every reaction we have is controlled by hiss power.

Even strong reactions and complaints can be mature actions, rather than temper tantrums. It is easy to identify the stages of development in the natural aspect, from childhood to adulthood. In the same way, there are stages from immaturity to maturity as children of God.

When the heart of a child of God is governed by Christ, their desire will be satisfied, and that will make sinful desires disappear, because what brings satisfaction to their life is Christ. But if your heart has areas that are not governed by Jesus, these areas will be immature and will be carried away by the desires of the flesh.

How can we realize that there is an area of our being that is not filled by Christ? The answer to this question is obtained by identifying the temptations that we recurringly give in to. The child of God who has allowed themself to be molded and filled by Christ will be someone who will act more like him. Thus, they will become a mature child.

It is interesting to note that the New Testament uses three words that are translated as "child" and whose meanings are related to maturity.

1. *TEKNION*

- It refers to the child who is small, who cannot fend for themselves and therefore depends on someone else. The Bible says that these children still need guardians because, although they are heirs, they cannot make their inheritance effective due to their immaturity. At this stage the word *nepios* is also used to refer to a small and immature child.

- In John 13:33 Jesus uses the word *teknion* for his disciples, making them see that they were just newborns, and they were not yet ready.

- In 1 John 2:1 the writer also uses the word *teknion* to refer to those of his disciples who still struggled with the same sins. Not to judge them, but to remind them that Christ has forgiven their sins, even though they are not yet able to avoid them.

2. *TEKNON*

- It refers to a child who has already gone through some processes and has taken growth steps. They have demonstrated based on their decisions and lifestyle that they not only follow Christ, but also have been willing to be formed by him.

- In Galatians 4:19 Paul uses the word *teknon* to refer to those spiritual children who had already developed to such an extent that their processes had caused Paul labor pains, alluding to the suffering caused by the formation of a spiritual child, that is, of a disciple. However, the *teknon* is not yet sufficiently mature.

- In Romans 9:8-11 Paul uses the word *teknon* to refer to those spiritual children who are maturing with respect to their purpose and are heading toward their calling.

3. *HUIOS*

- This is the type of child who has matured enough to take responsibility, having responded positively to their formation processes. They are a child who has acquired the mature criteria of the Father.

- In Luke 9:35, the voice of the Father that comes from heaven affirms the maturity of Jesus, the Son in whom he is pleased. There, the term *huios* is used.

- At the beginning of the account of the Gospel of Matthew, the same term is also used to refer to Jesus.

Disciples are in constant growth to be formed as mature children. A disciple is essentially a maturing child of God, someone who passes through the growth processes in which they are tested. From the beginning, when they receive simple tasks and sometimes fail to obey, until, as time goes by, they take steps of greater obedience that help them to mature.

An immature child cannot receive greater responsibilities from the Father. They still ask for food and shelter, and beg for protection, instead of confidently knowing that the Father will always provide, protect, and supply what is necessary, just as a mature child would think. An immature child still has to grow up, is selfish, questions everything, and the answers do not always satisfy them. A mature child accepts the will of the Father because they understand that he is greater, and infinite in wisdom.

A DISCIPLE IS ESSENTIALLY A MATURING CHILD OF GOD.

 INTROSPECTION

The best discipleship happens when disciples can do what their disciplers have shown them, not just out of obedience or imitation, but out of conviction. So now it is vital to go back to the assessment that was done at the beginning of the lesson.

We must remember and affirm the following:

- Character is part of a person's inner being.

- On the outside we can put on a false front, but what is in the heart reflects our true being.

- The more we let God mold our character, the better tools we will be in God's hands to fulfill his purposes.

- The more mature our character is, the more similar it will be to that of Jesus.

- The more mature we are, the more in control we are.

THE BEST DISCIPLESHIP HAPPENS WHEN DISCIPLES CAN DO WHAT THEIR DISCIPLERS HAVE SHOWN THEM, NOT JUST OUT OF OBEDIENCE OR IMITATION, BUT OUT OF CONVICTION.

REFLECTION QUESTIONS FOR THE GROUP

- What is the fate of a person who does not control their character?

- Is it possible to change the character? How can that happen?

- What areas of character are most difficult to change?

- What things can we learn from Jesus about his character?

REMEMBER

When the boys and girls in your group are sharing their ideas, there are no wrong answers. These moments are for them to know that they can talk without being judged, and for you to explore the way teens think. Don't stop or correct them; encourage them to keep talking even if you disagree with their assessments. Little by little, the Word of God will change them. Don't try to rush that process.

 REFLECT ON A CHARACTER

CHRIS BROWN

As it happens with any celebrity couple, the courtship of Rihanna and rapper Chris Brown had a lot of news to offer the press. Chris was arrested and tried for assaulting his girlfriend. He claimed that they were both struggling, and that in fact she was the one who became the most violent. He then tried to vindicate his actions, but the photographs that circulated on the news networks showing Rihanna's face after the violent encounter with her boyfriend did not make clearing his name an easy task.

The pressure on artists is much greater than just making sure they look good in photos. They are always on the lookout. Their successes bring joy to many, but their failures get a lot more press and cause people to spread rumors, criticize them, and judge them all the time. Taking a relationship to the point of physical aggression is something very common in many of these couples, and some even learn to live with it. However, that should never happen.

In the case of Chris Brown, the punches to his girlfriend's face were forceful, and no matter how many explanations he wants to offer, nothing justifies such a lack of self-control, no matter how angry he was feeling at the time.

QUESTION FOR THE DISCIPLES

- Why does violence arise between people who apparently love each other?

PETER

The Bible hides nothing, and it has not been a problem for any of the biblical writers to describe in full detail what really happened. This is another of the arguments that make the Word of God a reliable and true instrument.

Peter is perhaps the most famous apostle of all, and he didn't earn that position by always doing the right thing. Peter was impulsive. He had a difficult character to control, to the point that in a fit of anger he decided to cut off the ear of one of those who wanted to arrest his Master! A little later, it was Peter who denied Jesus three times, although before he had been quick to promise that he would never leave him alone.

However, it is said that Peter was very close to Jesus. From the day his spiritual eyes were opened and he became certain that Jesus was the Christ, everything in Peter's life changed. Peter had been an impetuous and strong fisherman, capable of shouldering all the hard work that his trade required. Because of that same strong character, Peter was the one who asked the questions that the others did not dare to ask, and he had more initiative than the rest of the disciples. All of that was positive, but as we saw, he also had to deal with aspects of his character that he couldn't seem to control.

QUESTIONS FOR THE DISCIPLES

- What kind of strong reactions like Peter's could we have today?

- How is it possible for us to take control if we have reactions like this?

- What should we imitate from Peter and what should we not?

 MOBILIZE

To close this lesson, choose a simple game in which your disciples can compete. It can be Ping-pong, a simple card game, or some sport that they can do in a small space. For this competition you will be the judge, but when awarding the points, you will use subjective criteria and you will constantly change the rules.

Conceal your actions a bit, but the point is to create some frustration with your constantly changing criteria and your "injustices." Make those who have a disadvantage win, and in another round make no one win even if they have achieved the objective. Turn it into a very unfair situation, and throughout the course of the game you will notice that an atmosphere of frustration is being generated, and that many will not be able to control their emotions. After a while, stop the game and admit what you were doing. Then allow them to talk and vent. This is the time to go through the entire lesson with firm steps towards a better future.

A mature character doesn't explode with frustration over a game and thinks of others and not just themself when they don't like a situation.

What do we do in the face of injustices then?

Learn to govern our emotions to face them adequately.

LESSON 4

DREAMS OF ATTRACTION

Wherever there is truth, there will be God.
Alex Sampedro, *Craftsman*

You may have seen the movie *Sierra Burgess is a Loser*, whose protagonist is a teenager who considers herself unattractive and who, due to her image, prefers to be hidden. With the help of a friend, she begins an online romance with a boy who is a good athlete and has a physical appearance that is envied by everyone; the perfect stereotype of what it means to be cool.

Can an unpopular and unattractive girl (according to social standards) win the heart of the stereotypical cool guy?

That's not the only movie that touches on these themes. Almost all the movies and TV shows that involve teenagers show the preoccupation with physical appearance and the dream of being cool. In real life, many adolescent conversations revolve around this topic, even if they don't always deal with it directly and don't always use the word "cool."

AVALANCHE OF IDEAS

Show your teens photos of two physically "attractive" people who you know have also been dangerous people. Two examples that you can search the web for are Andrea Yates and Aaron Hernandez. (You can search for their biographies on the web and choose the best photograph of each one.) The short version is that Andrea Yates drowned her five children, and Aaron Hernandez murdered his friend. Of course, you can find other more contemporary or national examples by searching. The point is that teenagers should not recognize them immediately.

When showing them the photos, ask them what kind of people they think they are. Invariably, if the photos show them attractive and smiling, your teenagers will assume they are good people. (Since we were little, we learn in the movies that the heroes are cute, and the bad guys are the ugly ones.)

Let them say what they think, and then tell them each of their stories. The idea of this activity is to spark a conversation about physical appearance and what it means to be "attractive" to teenagers.

SOME QUESTIONS:

- How important is it to look good?

- On a scale of 1 to 10, how much do we value physical beauty?

FOUNDATIONS OF THE THEME

Having a pleasant physical appearance and standing out at something are usually very strong aspirations during adolescence. Generally, because of their appearance or the activities they do, teenagers are placed in a certain group with "similar interests." Thus, there are "athletes," "musicians," "gamers," etc. Other groups include "the nerds" (as a stereotype of studious boys and girls), "the cool kids" (those who are most popular and admired by the whole school), and there is also usually a group for those who smoke or drink to show themselves as smarter than others.

We must understand that the tastes of teenagers, like the clothes they wear, are superficial aspects of identity. However, according to Dr. John Townsend in *Boundaries with Teens*, a teen's clothing can tell us a lot about their inner world:

"Inappropriate style of dressing may indicate a need for peer approval... a sensual style may indicate that the teen is relying more on her body than her character to attract boys... dark themes, such as death, drugs and violence may indicate internal alienation, anger or rebellion... The clothing that is culturally based, such as gang styles or colors, may express inappropriate values."

THE TASTES OF TEENAGERS, LIKE THE CLOTHES THEY WEAR, ARE SUPERFICIAL ASPECTS OF THEIR IDENTITY.

It's good to recognize this, not to put a label on your teenagers, but to better discern what they need.

Of course, it's not just clothing that gives us clues to teens' search for identity, but also their tastes in music, sports, and other activities. Even their favorite subjects or classes at school can show us the paths they are taking.

Another factor that we must consider is that, as teenagers have not yet reached full maturity in many areas of their lives, they are continuously searching, and it is part of our task to accompany them in this discovery process.

Furthermore, many of their attitudes are impulsive, and they do not always measure the consequences of their actions. However, it is not our job to tell them how they should dress, who they should look up to, or what they should become when they grow up. Our role as disciplers must be centered on accompanying them as they discover, through what is taught, the richness and depth of God's instruction in their lives. The key is that they can value what is correct, and not get carried away by the labels that the world decides to put on them.

Let us also remember that some of the tastes that the boys and girls in our group now manifest are likely linked to activities they will be involved in for the rest of their lives, but others are not. Focusing on passing interests that the majority don't care about is just wasting time and energy.

WE NEED TEACH TEENAGERS THAT MATURING IN THE RIGHT WAY WILL MAKE THEM LOOK ATTRACTIVE FROM THE INSIDE OUT!

Returning to the issue of physical appearance, we must bear in mind that in most cases the desire to feel attractive has to do not only with a cultural value, but also with wanting to attract someone, and can even be a survival instinct. In the TV show *100 Humans*, an interview was conducted with Dr. Jody Armour, a USC law professor, about what he calls "an unconscious prejudice" that makes us judge less harshly the people we find most attractive. The theory states that an unattractive perpetrator is more likely to receive a higher sentence than one who is attractive.

However, it is also important to analyze what we consider attractive, and why. In that same show, a test was carried out with the viewers, placing photographs of different people so that the most attractive of all was chosen. After the experiment, the directors of the program confessed that the image of the person whom the majority chose as the most attractive was the one who had been placed in front of the screens for the longest amount of time. That means it was the familiarity of his face that made this person get chosen.

Now imagine that your boys and girls could know that no matter how attractive they are by world and media standards or how good they feel with their physique, when choosing a partner in the future their personality, character, and values will carry more weight, as well as their closeness to the other person. In other words, we need to teach teenagers that maturing the right way will make them look attractive from the inside out!

📖 FOCUS ON TRUTH

Assign the discipleship group to read from John 18. It is important that everyone has read the entire chapter before beginning this discussion. You can ask them to do it at home before they arrive at the meeting, or you can take a few minutes to do it all together. Remember that if you want to do intense, long-term discipleship work, you can spend one, two, or even four weeks on each lesson, depending on how much time you want to spend on each topic.

John 18 is a key chapter regarding the identity of Jesus. There we see how the Master had to face questions from various people about who he really was, and he had to do this in three different places. Let's see how the story begins...

When he had finished praying, Jesus left with his disciples and crossed the Kidron Valley. On the other side there was a garden, and he and his disciples went into it.

Now Judas, who betrayed him, knew the place, because Jesus had often met there with his disciples.

So Judas came to the garden, guiding a detachment of soldiers and some officials from the chief priests and the Pharisees. They were carrying torches, lanterns, and weapons.

Jesus, knowing all that was going to happen to him, went out and asked them, "Who is it you want?"

"Jesus of Nazareth," they replied.

"I am he," Jesus said. (And Judas the traitor was standing there with them.) When Jesus said, "I am he," they drew back and fell to the ground.

Again he asked them, "Who is it you want?"

"Jesus of Nazareth," they said.

Jesus answered, "I told you that I am he. If you are looking for me, then let these men go." This happened so that the words he had spoken would be fulfilled: "I have not lost one of those you gave me."

Then Simon Peter, who had a sword, drew it and struck the high priest's servant, cutting off his right ear. (The servant's name was Malchus.)

Jesus commanded Peter, "Put your sword away! Shall I not drink the cup the Father has given me?"

John 18:1–11

First of all, we find in this passage that Jesus is in the garden of Gethsemane. The word Gethsemane, analyzed in its original language, means "oil press." That was the place where Jesus had to pass the hardest test in his earthly ministry. (You can study the parallel passages in the other Gospels so that you have more references about what that moment was like.) He would have liked not to have to die on a cross, because the suffering would be enormous, but he knew that he had to do it out of love for us and obedience to the Father.

What we see in this scene is that a company of soldiers and constables came to arrest Jesus with lighted torches, lamps, and weapons. They came prepared for a violent confrontation. They considered Jesus an outlaw, an enemy. But he went ahead to meet them on the road. "Who are you looking for?" he asked them, although he knew very well what they were coming for. "To Jesus of Nazareth," they answered. Then something unexpected happened. The one they thought was going to try to run away, hide, or at least make an attempt to fight, simply told them: "I am."

Notice that this was the same phrase that God had used to introduce himself to Moses in Exodus 3:14: "God said to Moses, "I AM WHO I AM. This is what you are to say to the Israelites: 'I AM has sent me to you."

Those who had asked this immediately fell backwards, we don't know if it's because of the surprise that he gave himself up that way, or because of the divine presence that Jesus radiated. The truth is that with these words Jesus was affirming who he was. His identity did not depend on his physical appearance, nor did it depend on the soldiers' threats or any other circumstance. He knew his purpose, his mission, and by whom he had been sent. Although they had come looking for him as if he were a criminal, the true identity of Jesus was expressed in his actions and in his words.

But we said we would talk about three places. The garden of Gethsemane was the first.

The second place where they took Jesus was before Annas, the high priest of the Jews, and father-in-law of Caiaphas. There, in the courtyard, they decided to question Jesus about who he was, about his disciples, and about his teachings:

"Then the detachment of soldiers with its commander and the Jewish officials arrested Jesus. They bound him and brought him first to Annas, who was the father-in-law of Caiaphas, the high priest that year. Caiaphas was the one who had advised the Jewish leaders that it would be good if one man died for the people...

Meanwhile, the high priest questioned Jesus about his disciples and his teaching.

"I have spoken openly to the world," Jesus replied. "I always taught in synagogues or at the temple, where all the Jews come together. I said nothing in secret. Why question me? Ask those who heard me. Surely they know what I said."

When Jesus said this, one of the officials nearby slapped him in the face. "Is this the way you answer the high priest?" he demanded.

"If I said something wrong," Jesus replied, "testify as to what is wrong. But if I spoke the truth, why did you strike me?" Then Annas sent him bound to Caiaphas the high priest.

John 18:12–14, 19–24

So sure was Jesus of who he was and what he had come to do that he did not need to justify himself in front of anyone! His response was powerful: "I have never hidden to speak; ask those who have heard me!"

While this was happening, Peter, the disciple who had promised to follow him to death, was also questioned about his identity. Many of those who saw him asked him: "You look like one of his disciples," "I think I saw you with them," "You were one of the twelve closest," To these three questions, Peter answered no. Then the rooster crowed, and Peter wept bitterly because Jesus had told him that this would happen.

This can lead us to another reflection. Peter denied Jesus even though a day before he was completely sure that he was going to follow him to death. How hard is it to stand firm in what we believe?

Going back to the biblical text, we already saw that the first place was the garden of Gethsemane. The second was before Annas and Caiaphas.

The third was the praetorium:

> Then the Jewish leaders took Jesus from Caiaphas to the palace of the Roman governor. By now it was early morning, and to avoid ceremonial uncleanness they did not enter the palace, because they wanted to be able to eat the Passover. So *Pilate came out to them and asked, "What charges are you bringing against this man?"*
>
> *"If he were not a criminal," they replied, "we would not have handed him over to you."*
>
> *Pilate said, "Take him yourselves and judge him by your own law."*
>
> *"But we have no right to execute anyone," they objected. This took place to fulfill what Jesus had said about the kind of death he was going to die.*
>
> *Pilate then went back inside the palace, summoned Jesus and asked him, "Are you the king of the Jews?"*
>
> *"Is that your own idea," Jesus asked, "or did others talk to you about me?"*
>
> *"Am I a Jew?" Pilate replied. "Your own people and chief priests handed you over to me. What is it you have done?"*
>
> *Jesus said, "My kingdom is not of this world. If it were, my servants would fight to prevent my arrest by the Jewish leaders. But now my kingdom is from another place."*
>
> *"You are a king, then!" said Pilate.*
>
> *Jesus answered, "You say that I am a king. In fact, the reason I was born and came into the world is to testify to the truth. Everyone on the side of truth listens to me."*

"What is truth?" retorted Pilate. With this he went out again to the Jews gathered there and said, "I find no basis for a charge against him. But it is your custom for me to release to you one prisoner at the time of the Passover. Do you want me to release 'the king of the Jews'?"

They shouted back, "No, not him! Give us Barabbas!" Now Barabbas had taken part in an uprising.

John 18:28-40

The praetorium was the residence of the Roman governor, Pontius Pilate. Jesus was brought there because the leaders of the Jews wanted his death sentence to come from Rome. In this palace, the governor also questioned Jesus about his identity. Even knowing that it was due to Caesar and the Roman Empire, Pilate hesitated to sentence this man to death, since he found no crime in him. "Are you the king of the Jews?" he asked him over and over again. And Jesus's answers were always accurate. "My kingdom is not of this world." "You say that I am a king." Thus, Jesus showed that he was sure of who he was. And on this last occasion he did it before the governor, a representative of Rome, of the Gentiles, and of the whole world.

Today, we are constantly being questioned about what we do, how we look, the way we dress, and how we behave. Only God knows our hearts, but we must be clear about our purpose and what we have come to this world to do. When that is clear, the rest loses importance, and then we know that we do not need to live or act to satisfy the questions of others, but to manifest what we have in our hearts.

INTROSPECTION

This is a good opportunity to help your teens explore their motivation for dressing or acting the way they do.

Using the same activity of the photographs, choose pictures of teenagers dressed in fashion at different historical times and with different current styles. Look for various examples, from the most bizarre to those that would go unnoticed.

Let them talk about it for a while with questions that facilitate the conversation:

- Which of all the styles did you most identify with?

- How would you feel dressing in some of these styles?

- What style of clothing would you never wear?

And if there is enough trust with your group, you can ask questions like:

- How do you feel about your body? (Include here different aspects such as weight, height, skin color, eyes, etc.)

- How do you think others see you?

- What things would you like to change in regard to your physical appearance?

(You can also use these questions for personal conversations.)

 REFLECT ON A CHARACTER

ADELE

British singer-songwriter Adele began receiving praise from everyone for her talent before she had even turned 20. From then on, her career exploded. She got millions and millions of downloads of her music all over the world and even received an Oscar and a Golden Globe for best original song for the theme of the movie *Skyfall*. Even the famous *Time* magazine recognized her by including her in the list of the hundred most influential people in the world when she was barely 25 years old.

Despite all this success, Adele was not confident with her figure and began a process of changing her diet and lifestyle, so much so that people began to worry about her and criticize her thinness. Adele lived through both dramas: as a teenager she suffered criticism for being overweight, and later, when she lost weight, criticism for her change of image.

QUESTIONS FOR THE DISCIPLES

- Why do you think people care so much about the physical image of other people?

- Why would someone as successful as Adele decide to lose weight?

JOHN THE BAPTIST

Jesus knew John from before he was born, when they were both in their mothers' wombs. Although Scripture does not mention much about his childhood and adolescence, it is very likely that, as the son of Mary's cousin, John was someone very close to Jesus in his childhood years. Once reaching adulthood, John reappears in the Bible and a brief, but rather striking description is made of him. You can find it in the story of Jesus's baptism in the Gospels of Matthew, Mark, and Luke.

Here is Matthew's version:

In those days John the Baptist came, preaching in the wilderness of Judea and saying, "Repent, for the kingdom of heaven has come near." This is he who was spoken of through the prophet Isaiah:

"A voice of one calling in the wilderness, 'Prepare the way for the Lord, make straight paths for him.'"

John's clothes were made of camel's hair, and he had a leather belt around his waist. His food was locusts and wild honey.

People went out to him from Jerusalem and all Judea and the whole region of the Jordan. Confessing their sins, they were baptized by him in the Jordan River.

Matthew 3:1–6

John was a traveling preacher, and his biggest setting was the desert. His clothes were made of camel hair, and his food was wild honey and locusts. This description clearly makes us think that he was a person that the rest would consider "strange." His clothes and food were not common in his time, nor was his way of living in the desert like a hermit. His preaching was harsh, but nevertheless John led many to repent and turn to God, which was necessary because this man came to prepare the way for the arrival of the Messiah.

It is interesting that John did not seem to care about his image, or what others might think of him. John cared more about his purpose; that for which he had been called by God. Most likely, many people spoke ill of him behind his back, but that didn't stop him at all! John was so committed to his call that he decided to ignore any of the strategies the enemy used to try to stop him.

The example of John the Baptist is powerful. It reminds us that the most important thing is to focus passionately on the purpose that God has placed before us, and that this makes us attractive in the eyes of God and also of others.

QUESTIONS FOR THE DISCIPLES

- In what way can our image become more important than our purpose?

- What example do you think John the Baptist gives us?

MOBILIZE

From this lesson, we want the teens participating in this discipleship project to make a less superficial evaluation of others and of themselves. Here are some actions to challenge them:

- Value people who at first glance are not so attractive.

- Don't put attractive and popular people above others who are not.

- Spend more energy on being a better person than on looking good. (Taking care of how you look is fine, but it is not good for that to become more important than trying to be a better person.)

- Work on how other people see you, but don't get anxious about pleasing people who judge you at first sight.

- Clearly define what inner beauty is all about.

- Live with purpose instead of for your appearance.

SEXUAL INTELLIGENCE

If you feed your mind with negative influences, the negative will come out. If you feed it positive messages, then the positive will win.

Lucas Leys and Jim Burns, *The purity code*

We live in a hypersexualized society, and it is very difficult to escape the continuous sexual provocation and confusion that today's teenagers are exposed to.

Although parents and leaders want to be always present with our children or disciples, neither will be able to enter their minds. That is why it is vital that each disciple learns to take control of their convictions regarding sexuality and their exposure to wrong ideas and temptations that come from outside.

SEXUALITY IS AN ASPECT OF IDENTITY, AND THEREFORE IS A VITALLY IMPORTANT ISSUE DURING ADOLESCENCE.

Sexuality is an aspect of identity, and therefore it is a vitally important issue during adolescence.

 AVALANCHE OF IDEAS

The rating system that determines what images are suitable for each age in cinema and television is different in each country, so look for the classification that is used in your country to carry out the following activity.

Here, for example, is a general ratings system:

CODE	ALTERNATIVE	MEANING	MOVIES
A	G	For all ages. No sexual content, no nudity, no (or little) presence of drugs, alcohol, or tobacco, and minimal violence. There may be nonviolent or explicit deaths. Polite language.	
B	PG	Restricted for children under 10, 12, or 13 years old depending on the country, with adult supervision. Partial nudity, non-violent deaths, and blood. The language can be risqué.	
C	PG-13	Some nudity. Alcohol, drugs, insults, violent deaths, and a lot of blood. It should not be viewed by persons under 13 years of age.	
D	R (18)	Restricted to persons under 18 years of age. (In some places identification is requested to verify age.) Strong nudity and explicit sex scenes.	

Ask your teens to share their impressions of this chart using the following questions: Is it a fair classification? Is there any aspect that should be improved? If so, which one(s)?

Let them talk and then challenge them to put themselves in the parenting position with this question: If you were a mom or dad, what would you and wouldn't you let your kids see?

If you have access to the internet during the meeting, ask the group to research some of the movies they would choose to see, or have already seen. Then ask them to look at the rating of those movies or TV shows. Fill the space in the right column of the chart above with the movies that your disciples name.

With this column complete, pick up the conversation.

 FOUNDATIONS OF THE THEME

The influence we receive from the environment means that little by little we build our convictions about every aspect of life. If a teenager grows up in a family that places a high value on academic training, it is very likely that a lot of their attention is focused there. If, on the other hand, you grow up in an environment where the arts are very important, that influence will surely be evident in your adult life.

The same thing happens with sexuality. Everything that a child sees, hears, and perceives with their senses, they store in their brain. In a home in which adults have not taken any precautions regarding what children and teenagers watch on the internet, it is most likely that they have been exposed to many stimuli that are inappropriate for their age without even realizing it. In these cases, since they grew up seeing it as something normal, it becomes part of their culture.

The other extreme is interesting too. If the child or adolescent has been deprived of seeing almost everything, without any type of explanation or analysis of the reason for these restrictions, an unconscious desire to see what they have been prohibited from seeing is generated in their mind. If you don't know exactly what your parents are protecting you from, sooner or later you will end up looking for it without proper criteria, just because fear of parents will no longer be part of your system by the time you go to college.

By God's design, the body prepares for sexual life after puberty, so it is inevitable (and even desirable) that teenagers have questions about sexuality. The problem is that the disordered stimuli of pornography speak of sexuality as only a form of physical pleasure, disconnecting it from the social, emotional, spiritual, and even physiological implications. That is why it is vital to teach them that God created sex to be enjoyed intelligently, and not as a hormonal outlet that harms us.

SEX IS LIKE FIRE. IT IS WONDERFUL FOR ITS POSITIVE USES, BUT EXTREMELY DANGEROUS WHEN IT GETS OUT OF HAND.

Sex is like fire. It is wonderful for its positive uses, but extremely dangerous when it gets out of hand. Why? Because sex is intimately linked to identity, and sharing our identity in such an intimate way with someone implies having a connection with that person for the rest of our lives. That is why the Bible and science confirm that the best expression of sexuality occurs in the full commitment of marriage.

One of the most important things to discuss with your teens when talking about sexuality is the subject of pornography. You can go as deep as the group allows, but the first thing you should share with the group is that in an addiction to pornography, the following sequence can be observed:

1. The person views pornography, perhaps casually or out of curiosity.

2. An intentional search is initiated.

3. The search intensifies and the addiction begins, since the person finds it almost impossible to stop the search.

4. Insensitivity to soft porn arrives. The things that the person has seen no longer give them the same satisfaction as before, so they begin a search for new forms of pornography to feel that satisfaction again.

5. The brain is captive with actions of twisted sex that drive twisted desires. (This sequence is well known to those who produce pornography, and for this reason they play with fantasy.)

6. Sexual acts. All this search for sexual sensations makes the person finally end up going to places or looking for people to make their fantasies come true.

As you can see, at first pornography is related to a habit. However, it does not stop there, because the brain and human body are designed to make the person feel more and more desire and seek variety. Hence, the problem intensifies, and in a short time it produces insensitivity in the person, since the images and scenes that previously brought them satisfaction no longer do so. For this reason, they begin to look for new and more intense ways to quench the sexual thirst that pornography has produced, until reaching a moment in which the person tries to make reality what, until now, has only been experienced in fiction.

This process can develop very quickly but getting rid of it is not easy. Some, in fact, fight their entire lives against this poison that contaminates God's beautiful design. Falling into pornography is not smart, and therefore it is necessary that we alert our teenagers about this danger that lies in wait for them. It is very easy to fall into an addiction to pornography, and adolescence is precisely the time to work to avoid it.

They must learn that their most powerful sexual organ is not one that is covered by a bathing suit.

The ultimate key to sex is not between the legs, but between the ears, which is why it is vital that teenagers learn God's plan for sexuality and the great danger of sexual disorders.

📖 FOCUS ON TRUTH

Read the following verses together:

> *The one who does what is sinful is of the devil, because the devil has been sinning from the beginning. The reason the Son of God appeared was to destroy the devil's work. No one who is born of God will continue to sin, because God's seed remains in them; they cannot go on sinning, because they have been born of God.*
>
> **1 John 3:8–9**

Christians still struggle with sin, but we have turned our backs on it and are no longer enslaved to its power. Some have explained this by pointing to the difference between falling from time to time and practicing sin continuously. Others put the emphasis on the intention or direction of your heart. Do you passionately desire to live in holiness?

While it is true that we remain human, imperfect, and fallible, we must trust that what Scripture says is real, and actively join Jesus in destroying the works of the devil.

Remember, once again, that this is a PROCESS. It does not happen by force, but by the progressive knowledge of God.

God's design for sexuality is clear. Review the following verses with your group:

- "God blessed them and said to them, 'Be fruitful and increase in number; fill the earth and subdue it'" (Genesis 1:28). God created sexuality for the multiplication of the human race. It is the way in which God arranged the physical fruit that we can bear as human beings. If it were so bad, it would not produce growth but extinction.

- "Drink water from your own cistern, running water from your own well. Should your springs overflow in the streets, your streams of water in the public squares? Let them be yours alone, never to be shared with strangers" (Proverbs 5:15-17). God designed sexuality for the delight of the spouses. Sexual delight is not wrong or sinful when it occurs within God's design, which is marriage. Outside of it, sex produces guilt and condemnation.

- "'For this reason a man will leave his father and mother and be united to his wife, and the two will become one flesh.' This is a profound mystery—but I am talking about Christ and the church" (Ephesians 5:31-32). Here we see that Paul relates the union between a man and his wife to the union of Christ and the church. Sure, it's a mystery that we still can't understand, but the parallelism that exists is phenomenal! And we are talking about unity in all areas of life: physical, emotional, affective, mental, spiritual. There is no such unity if sex is used outside the scope for which God created it!

In short, it is clear that God had something good in mind when he designed sexuality. And although today society has so corrupted the original concept of what sex should be, it is our duty as children of God and as disciples of Jesus to recover the true meaning that God planned for this.

INTROSPECTION

Now help them think by asking some questions:

- What do you think our boundaries should be when it comes to watching movies and TV shows?

- Who or what determines when to have sexual intercourse? Why?

- What should we do when we are in a group where everyone thinks differently from what we know to be correct?

Allow them to discuss and debate the above questions for a while. Then let them know what you expect of them in dealing with this topic. You should post these goals prominently on a whiteboard or piece of paper for everyone to see.

Here are some ideas, but feel free to include your own:

- I hope this group is smart enough to handle their sexuality in the right way.

- I hope you know how to discern between what is good for you and what is harmful to you.

- I hope to one day see you making good decisions regarding your relationships.

- I hope you will seek help when you feel stuck.

Now let's talk a little about diseases. It never hurts to talk about diseases.

An alarming statistic regarding STDs (sexually transmitted diseases) is presented in Josh McDowell's book *The Naked Truth*:

- 1 in 4 sexually active teenagers is infected with STDs.

- 70 million Americans are currently living with an STD.

- 65 million of those cases have no cure.

- Around the world, 330 million people contract an STD each year.

Some questions to think about:

- What are the main STDs that exist in the world today?

- How much do my teens know about them and their consequences?

- How much information do the parents of my teenagers have in order to talk to their children about it?

- How much knowledge about these topics do the pastors and leaders of the congregation have?

Instilling fear in our teens so that they will stay away from unsafe sex is always an incomplete task, so be careful that the conversation does not stop with the fear. What we need is to put intelligence in their decisions, as these decisions will affect their destination.

The expression "sexual intelligence" contains two words that are apparently unrelated to each other. However, today more than ever, we need to unite them. During adolescence we have to help our brain make decisions related to sexuality, because sexuality without intelligence is too high a risk.

Another aspect of disordered sexual relations is the scarce and biased information regarding condoms, which are the most popular contraceptive method in the world. Although it is said that condoms offer a high degree of protection to prevent pregnancy and avoid contracting STDs, the truth is that even with the use of condoms there is a huge risk of acquiring a sexually transmitted disease or becoming pregnant. This means that your protection is not complete, but only partial. In addition, it must be taken into account that some STDs can also be transmitted through genital contact and caresses, despite the use of condoms. This doesn't sound like complete protection, does it?

In case you want more details, in a study that the condom manufacturing companies were forced to carry out, it was found that the percentage of "error" or "failure" that condoms have as a method to prevent pregnancy is 31%. This is a much larger number than advertised in the commercials!

SEXUALITY WITHOUT INTELLIGENCE IS TOO HIGH A RISK.

It is necessary to warn our teenagers that the use of condoms is not as smart as we have been led to think, and that the best way to keep our bodies healthy and avoid any risk of unwanted or early pregnancy is abstinence. Now that's smart!

Author Neil Anderson writes in the book *A Way of Escape*: "God doesn't command us to do something we can't do, or the devil can stop us from doing. In Christ you have died to sin, and the devil can do nothing to you. He will tempt you, accuse you and try to deceive you, but if sin reigns in your body, it is because you have allowed it to do so. You are responsible for your own attitudes and actions."

Being responsible for our own actions is one of the signs of maturity and character development.

 REFLECT ON A CHARACTER

JONAS BROTHERS

Kevin, Joe, and Nick Jonas formed what became one of the most popular boy bands in the world. Their career skyrocketed with many hits for several years until they decided to break up as a band and do solo work, until they united again.

It may be unknown to many, but in the beginning the Jonas Brothers spoke openly about their faith and, amid mountains of interviews and the madness of their world tours, they told all their fans about the decision they had made about sex. They had pledged before God to remain pure until marriage, sealing that pact with a ring that the three of them proudly displayed every time they were asked about it.

The pact that they made of obedience to God was worthy of being recognized, and for this act they were admired by many people, although many others never believed in that decision of the young singers. We cannot know if the three of them have managed to fulfill that pact, but having faced the entire world, while still teenagers, and in the midst of such a hypersexualized artistic world, surely deserves some credit.

QUESTIONS FOR THE DISCIPLES

- Why would the Jonas Brothers make this pact?

- What is the benefit and what is the price of making a covenant with God in this area?

SAMSON

Samson appears in the Bible in the book of Judges, from chapter 13 onwards.

The different facets of this character are extreme. From conception, he was chosen by God to be anointed as a Nazirite. As such, he had to comply with certain requirements, such as never cutting his hair, not drinking wine or cider, not touching dead animals, and a whole list of mandates that he had to adhere to in order to keep his vow.

Unfortunately, later in his life, Samson did the exact opposite. He killed a lion with his bare hands, thus touching a dead animal. And with a jawbone that he took from a dead donkey, he killed a thousand men. How clumsy! And while it is true that the manifestation of his strength was amazing, his inability to manage his emotions made him a very foolish man.

In chapter 14 you can see his obstinacy in marrying a woman whose name Scripture does not even mention. In chapter 15, you may be surprised to learn that Samson slept with a prostitute. However, probably the biggest mistake he made was contemplating taking Delilah as his wife, which is described in chapter 16. Delilah deceived Samson once, twice, and even three times, guided by the advice from the princes of the Philistines, who wanted to trap him. He thought he had everything under control, since he had not fallen for Delilah's tricks on those three occasions, but the fourth time he was not so lucky. Samson was tricked once more, telling Delilah the secret of his strength. Consequently, he not only lost his hair, but also his eyes and his freedom.

QUESTIONS FOR THE DISCIPLES

- Why couldn't Samson keep himself pure?

- What was the price he paid?

- What does staying pure look like today?

MOBILIZE

To define the next steps, these questions can be useful:

- How do we avoid sexual temptations with intelligence?

- How can I help my friends to keep us all pure?

- What should I consider about my sexuality in the formation of my identity?

- How is sexuality related to my future?

Affirm in your teenagers the conviction that they were made for purity, and that it is the best avenue toward joy and even sexual well-being.

Affirm in them the certainty that God wants them to enjoy their sexuality in a healthy way and that is why the wisest thing is to wait for the sacred bond of marriage.

Affirm in them the commitment to take practical steps to fight temptations with intelligence.

LESSON 6

THE FUNDAMENTAL CONNECTION

God doesn't call us to be comfortable.
He calls us to trust in Him.

Francis Chan, *Crazy Love*

Neo lives in a fictional world, an environment generated by computers that are connected with thick wires to your brain to make you experience all kinds of sensations and experiences that seem like reality and make you believe that you are in it. Morpheus has been looking for the "chosen one" for decades, because the prophecy says that this person will be able to save all of humanity, and he thinks that Neo is the one he has been looking for all these years. The trilogy begins with the search for and release of Neo from the machine system. Morpheus explains that he has been connected to a machine all his life and gives him the option to stay there or free himself from that slavery. He will only have to choose between the red and the blue pill.

The Matrix was the trilogy of films that launched a little-known Keanu Reeves to stardom at the time and caused, among other things, many to think about how contemporary society is so connected to the news and entertainment networks that they can make us experience what they want us to.

Who or what are our teens connected to through digital media?

The ideas, information, and influences that the disciples connect to will have everything to do with their aspirations and values, which is why this is a key issue. In adolescence it is vital that they understand the importance of knowing who they choose to walk near them and who to listen to. On the other hand, the fundamental connection that they must have is with the Father, through Christ. Without that connection, their life in the church will be meaningless.

THOSE WHO REGULARLY ATTEND CHURCH, CONGREGATE FAITHFULLY, AND FOLLOW CHRISTIAN PRACTICES MIGHT STILL BE MORE CONNECTED TO THE WORLD THAN TO GOD.

Being connected to the Matrix could mean being connected to the world, and many of them are in that situation. Even those who regularly attend church, congregate faithfully, and follow Christian practices might still be more connected to the world than to God.

AVALANCHE OF IDEAS

Get a long enough ball of yarn and some chairs, considering the number of participants there will be.

The first step will be to circle up, pass the ball of yarn around in random order, and ask each of the boys and girls to make a big knot or loop with the portion of yarn that they receive as they accept the ball. Ask them to leave a large space of unknotted yarn between one participant and another. Let there be at least six feet of space between people.

Once all the yarn is connected between the participants, the challenge will be that the entire group must travel from one point of the room to another (could be one end of the room to the other) without getting caught in the yarn. Create a difficult pathway that they will have to travel across to get to their destination. A second level is to do this while only walking on chairs. The one who touches the floor will not be able to continue; they will exit the game, and a chair will be removed.

The other rule is that each one must take the knot they made with one of their hands, and they cannot let go of it. It's not enough that you keep holding on to the rope or yarn; you must grab the knot you made on it. Whoever loosens the knot they made must leave, and a chair will also be removed in this case.

As you will soon see, the challenge is gradually getting more complicated. Be rigid in the rules. If someone touches the ground or someone lets go of the knot they made, they must exit the game.

Recommend that they think of a strategy, and that they talk to each other to organize themselves. The less they talk, the harder it will be to finish successfully!

If you wish, you can set a time limit to make it more intense.

OUTCOME

The most important part of this curious experience is the conclusion.

Gather the group together and ask them to share what they felt while playing the game. Ask them if they were successful or not, and why they think that was. Allow everyone to share their thoughts.

Now it's your time to bring home what just happened.

The yarn represents God. Without him we cannot live. That is why it was so necessary to be holding it at all times. But the knots were also important, because they represent each person who helps you get closer to God, such as leaders, mentors, earthly parents, spiritual parents, pastors, etc.

The chairs represent the difficulties of the path that one goes through and the decisions that are made in life. Sometimes they make you fall.

It makes clear the concept that we cannot move forward in life without holding hands with God, and we cannot do it without the company of people who help us stay firm on this path.

📝 FOUNDATIONS OF THE THEME

Admitting the existence of God is one thing, but trusting in him is another. According to Scripture, even the demons believe, although they flee when they hear his name. Therefore, believing is not enough. Trusting in God has more power. It has to do with a relationship that we can nurture. It's the same as what happens with a person you barely know; as you spend time together, you get to know each other more.

How do you connect with a new friend?

ADMITTING THE EXISTENCE OF GOD IS ONE THING, BUT TRUSTING IN HIM IS ANOTHER.

At first, someone tells you about a person, or they introduce you to them. You like that person, and you decide to look for moments to relate more with them. There is still no connection at this stage, you just spend time together, get to know each other more, and start to see what you have in common. If both continue to encourage the friendship, you will soon find more personal moments, learn to resolve conflicts, and, if all that goes well, you will have learned to stay connected with each other. On the other hand, if that connection does not occur well, friendship will remain as something fleeting, like memories of someone you once knew.

To connect with God we also have to go through some stages, which could be summarized as follows:

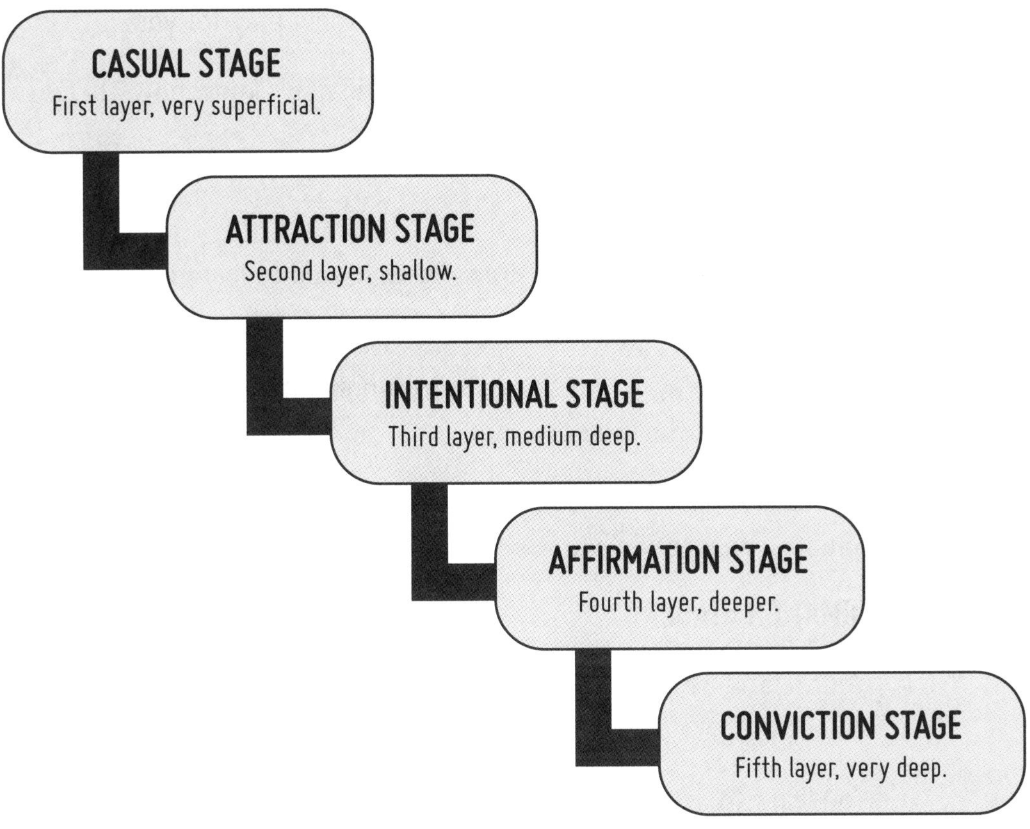

Here are the details of each stage:

1. CASUAL STAGE

◊ Someone told you about God or introduced you to the gospel.

◊ You still don't understand why those who follow God do what they do.

◊ Your life goes on the same as before, and there is no real connection with God.

2. ATTRACTION STAGE

◊ The gospel caught your attention, and you feel motivated to learn more about the God they are talking about.

◊ You don't know how to pray, but you let them pray for you.

◊ You want to change your life, but you still don't know how. There is no real connection with God.

3. **INTENTIONAL STAGE**

◊ You decide to intentionally draw closer to God to learn more about his Word.

◊ You learn to pray, to worship, and to congregate with others who think and feel the same.

◊ You have already changed some areas that were not good for you. You initiate a connection with God, but you put some conditions on it.

4. **AFFIRMATION STAGE**

◊ Your relationship with God is affirmed and becomes a genuine faith. You investigate deeply the things of God.

◊ You learn to listen to his voice. Prayer becomes a lifestyle, and you gain new ways of communicating with God.

◊ You put all your effort into changing your life and pleasing God. You are connected with God, and you decide to believe despite not understanding many things.

5. **CONVICTION STAGE**

◊ There will be nothing to change your way of thinking. You will follow God to the ends of the earth.

◊ You have a fluid communication with God, you know him through his Word and his voice, and you learn to see God in all things.

◊ You do not live in sin, but you move away from it. Your connection with God runs deep and you motivate others to have a close relationship with him.

Part of the path of a disciple is to navigate these waters. Try to identify which stage you are in. Then ask your boys and girls what stage they are at and share some ideas on how to progress to the next stages.

📖 FOCUS ON TRUTH

There is no better example in the Bible of connecting with God than that of Jesus. Throughout the Gospels we see him connected with the Father to make the important decisions. From his childhood to the moment of his last breath of natural life, Jesus did everything to please God.

The connection of Jesus with the Father and his will was noted in his prayers, in his speeches (which always ended by referring to the words that the Creator had inspired the ancient prophets to write), in his miracles (after which he always gave glory to the Father), and even when he talked about everyday things and shared with his disciples, since his words and actions showed that he had an intimate relationship with God.

THERE IS NO BETTER EXAMPLE IN THE BIBLE OF CONNECTING WITH GOD THAN THAT OF JESUS.

Show this sequence to your discipleship group:

- When he was a child, at 12 years old...

"Why were you searching for me?" he asked. "Didn't you know I had to be in my Father's house? **(Luke 2:49)**

...Jesus was certain that the Father wanted him there, in his affairs.

- At his baptism, before beginning his public ministry...

When all the people were being baptized, Jesus was baptized too. And as he was praying, heaven was opened and the Holy Spirit descended on him in bodily form like a dove. And a voice came from heaven: "You are my Son, whom I love; with you I am well pleased." **(Luke 3:21–22)**

...The Father's words affirmed the connection between them.

- In the choice of his disciples...

One of those days Jesus went out to a mountainside to pray, and spent the night praying to God. When morning came, he called his disciples to him and chose twelve of them, whom he also designated apostles: Simon (whom he named Peter), his brother Andrew, James, John, Philip, Bartholomew, Matthew, Thomas, James son of Alphaeus, Simon who was called the Zealot, Judas son of James, and Judas Iscariot, who became a traitor. **(Luke 6:12–16)**

...who spent the whole night praying? Jesus.

- When he teaches them to pray...

He said to them, "When you pray, say: 'Father, hallowed be your name, your kingdom come. Give us each day our daily bread. Forgive us our sins, for we also forgive everyone who sins against us. And lead us not into temptation.'" **(Luke 11:2–4)**

...the Father was always in his prayers.

- At the moment of his death...

Jesus called out with a loud voice, "Father, into your hands I commit my spirit." When he had said this, he breathed his last. **(Luke 23:46)**

...Jesus spoke with certainty that he was about to reunite with the Father.

...his way of expressing himself, of addressing the Father, of being one with him, and of asking us to also be one with him, all this makes us see the level of connection that Jesus had with the eternal God. Let's learn from Christ, our greatest example!

🛠 INTROSPECTION

It's time to get your disciples' neurons firing with some questions:

- In a general sense, what is religion?

- What is spirituality?

- What's the difference between the two?

When you open this discussion, you will find a lot of varying answers. You will see those who claim to be spiritual, but not religious. There may also be those who are faithful to a religion because they learned it that way. You will meet those who claim to be spiritual but, in reality, like the Pharisees, they practice the rituals of a religion but without a changed life. Some will tell you that Christianity is relationship and not a religion but they do not know why, and there will be those who say that without religion we would not know God.

WITHOUT A CHANGE IN DIRECTION OF OUR HEARTS, EXTERNAL RELIGION IS MEANINGLESS.

The truth is that without a change in direction of our hearts, external religion is meaningless. And even our genuine heart changes do not come by understanding God's grace, but as a natural and grateful reaction to that grace. It doesn't matter how much value you place on a religion, or how zealously you follow its practices; if you don't have a real connection with God, that religion ends up being useless. On the other hand, if you claim to be spiritual, you are in no place to judge religion, since your own spirituality makes you comply with the practices of religion.

What happened with the Pharisees is that they valued the religion that was seen more than their personal relationship with God. That is why they ended up with an empty religion, full of instructions that asked for obedience without understanding why.

 # REFLECT ON A CHARACTER

CANDACE CAMERON BURE

Candace was the protagonist of the TV show *Full House* and its sequel *Fuller House*, which became a super-successful show in the United States and other parts of the world. You can see Candace in interviews speaking openly about God and the importance of faith in her daily life, and demonstrating without any reserve that despite the fact that show business is full of temptations and counter-values, she has been able to stand firm.

It cannot be categorically assured what the level of her relationship with God is, nor at what stage it may be, since only God knows her heart. However, it is admirable to see the firmness when speaking of her convictions openly, even on complicated topics such as homosexuality and sin. She could stay silent, but she doesn't.

Her story contrasts with that of many Christians who try to go unnoticed in the world, in their schools, at their universities, in their jobs... and thus, little by little, they become more friendly with the world that surrounds them. This is very common but not ideal. As children of God, and as disciples of Christ, we should have the guts to say who we are. Although, thinking about it, the problem may not be in saying it but in being really convinced of it and acting according to who we really are.

SAMUEL

The prophet Samuel, writer of two books of the Bible, is considered a servant who was in constant connection with the eternal God. From a very young age he already heard God's voice, and although he did not know who God was or how to distinguish that voice, little by little he learned. Thanks to his sensitivity to hear the voice of God, Samuel was able to follow the instructions that came from God at all times, from things that seemed to be insignificant, to the prophetic acts of greatest relevance to the history of the people of God.

For example, Samuel received direction from God to anoint Saul as Israel's first king, and he also knew when it was time to remove him for his disobedience. He was able to find David to anoint him as Saul's successor even though he was out in the field herding sheep. Even when he was first introduced to all of David's brothers, Samuel knew to wait for the right one to arrive, the one whom God had chosen.

Samuel witnessed many battles, both victories and defeats, and nothing kept him from the God he had known since childhood. For Samuel, being connected with God meant not only listening to him, but also obeying him, and for this reason Samuel always had the privilege of hearing the audible voice of God that never faded throughout his life.

QUESTIONS FOR THE DISCIPLES

- What can we learn from these characters?

- How can they help us connect with God while disconnecting from the world?

MOBILIZE

Show your teens the relationship stages chart and help them assess where they are in their connection to God today, so they can to take the next step.

THE KEY TO GROWTH IS NOT IN JUMPING FROM THE FIRST LEVEL TO THE LAST, BUT IN MOVING ON TO THE NEXT LEVEL.

The key to growth is not in jumping from the first level to the last, but in moving on to the next level. For some that step will mean one thing, and for others, something else, so help them take concrete steps of growth from where each one is.

Develop a plan with them to continue advancing in the process. The plan may include some general ideas such as the following:

- Such as learn to listen to the voice of God in silence.

- Go out to a high place, such as a mountain, or the roof of a house or building (as long as it's safe) early in the morning to watch the sunrise. It may be that each one goes on their own, or that they get together to do it.

- Listen to a song one night of the week alone in their room and try to receive what God wants to say to them. You can suggest some songs to them for this.

- Gather for a time of prayer together, in person or virtually, at a time other than your regular meeting time.

- Organize a Bible reading challenge during the week. (At the end you can ask them to write, on paper or in a chat, what they feel they have received and heard from God personally.)

There are many other options too. The important thing is that the experience is a new step. This is part of the job of helping a disciple to further their intellectual knowledge of God.

ROMANCE AND DATING

The fact that something feels urgent and is natural does not justify that we do it without thought.

Lucas Leys, *Different*

What is the most repeated theme in movies and songs? There is no doubt that it is love. Music, paintings, sculptures, novels, television series, movies, and every aspect of the arts invites us to talk about love in some way. And it doesn't matter if it's summer, winter, autumn, or spring. If it's raining or sunny, all environments lend themselves to talking about love.

Your teenagers know this, and there is probably no other subject that fills them with more intrigue than this, and that is why it is vital to treat it wisely.

Love is the fabric of life because God is love. Romance and dating must be the prelude to the most beautiful and powerful expression of human commitment.

LOVE IS THE FABRIC OF LIFE BECAUSE GOD IS LOVE.

Talking about romance will trigger different reactions among teens. Some will look embarrassed because it's not a topic they would talk about openly if they had a choice; others will feel a sense of urgency; a few, misunderstood; and some may feel defeated. But what is certain is that everyone needs a clear, biblical, loving, and wise perspective on romance and dating.

🧠 AVALANCHE OF IDEAS

Assign each teen a role to play and have them answer the question in character.

What is love?

- A popular artist (you can choose different genres to facilitate more participation).

- A non-believing psychiatrist.

- A writer of romantic novels.

- A university student with a lot of money.

- A husband or wife who has been married for 30 years.

You can invent more characters, since there must be as many roles as you have disciples in your meeting.

The purpose of this activity is to explore teenagers' ideas about love from the perspective of others. This activity, like all the ones in this section of "Avalanche of Ideas," does not have the objective of drawing conclusions, nor of saying which theory is true or false, but simply of entering the topic and observing the way teenagers think, in this case from their theatrical performances. They will surely have fun!

After listening to each one without correcting them (so they don't say what they think you want to hear), celebrate the performances, and ask them the reasons why they acted in the specific way they did, or said what they chose to say.

📝 FOUNDATIONS OF THE THEME

Some people say that since the words "falling in love" do not exist in the Bible, we should not allow teenagers to fall in love. But if we are arguing about words that do not exist in the Bible, America is not in there, and we wouldn't say that it is unbiblical to live in America!

Let us also remember that whoever leads a discipleship project is not the one who tells the participants what to do, but someone who helps them to think in the most Christlike way while accompanying them on their walk through that process.

LOVE MEANS SEEKING THE MAXIMUM WELL-BEING OF THE OTHER PERSON.

Teenage emotions are real and normal. We should not condemn them for something that was designed by God in the expectation of a relationship. What we must do as disciplers is help teenagers manage their emotions wisely so that they are able to distinguish the opportune time for each thing.

Falling in love is a powerful feeling of attraction that explodes within a teenager, regardless of how reasonable that feeling is, creating a fanciful illusion about what life would be like with that person. When a boy or girl is excited, they start a whole imaginary process of idealized expectation about what a romantic approach with that other could mean. There is nothing wrong with it. In fact, it is not only normal but necessary to develop your personal conviction about love, and your ability to manage emotions and sensations.

In her book *Amar es para Valientes* (Love Is for the Brave), Itiel Arroyo paraphrases the apostle Paul saying that: "Love means seeking the maximum well-being of the other person, even above personal well-being." This notion about love is more urgent today than ever, because teenagers are often bombarded with messages that tell them that love is a feeling and that if the sensations are strong, it is because "chemistry" is there for the couple.

In fact, if you pay attention to popular songs and movies, you can easily identify the following 3 misconceptions about romantic love:

- **To love is to be happy.** This is what the TV shows and movies display, but true love definitely does not pursue personal satisfaction or your own happiness.

- **Having sex is making love.** The best proof of love is to want the best sexuality for the other person, and not the satisfaction of my desires. Sexual attraction is physical, and it is not synonymous with love.

- **Love is a feeling.** Although feelings are a beautiful part of love, feelings depend on circumstances, and even the most idealistic love at some point deflates emotions, especially from the commitment in the relationship. True love loves even when it doesn't feel it.

WHAT TRUE LOVE REALLY DOES

- **Prioritizes the happiness of the other**. The person who truly loves must be willing to give up their own happiness in order to make someone else happy.

- **Respects intimacy**. One who truly loves knows that they must save moments of intimacy until the right time arrives. No one who loves requires the other to go beyond what they are comfortable with.

- **Commits to the long term.** A couple's relationship was designed to be long-term, exclusive, and focused on a future together. But this future is something that is built little by little, and there is no relationship without problems. It is necessary to learn to go through difficult times together.

The next question we need to answer is: Is adolescence the ideal stage for romantic relationships?

If adolescence is the time to discover ourselves, it is not the best time to commit to another person who is also discovering themself.

One thing is certain. If we don't teach this generation sound principles about relationships, and if we don't teach them what to expect when it comes to dating, the results can be disastrous. But if we care enough to guide them toward relationships with a divine purpose, we will have better marriages and generations with a greater understanding of God and his will!

ADOLESCENCE IS THE STAGE WHERE I GET TO KNOW MYSELF, WHO I WANT TO BE, AND TO BEGIN TO CONSIDER WHAT KIND OF PERSON I WANT TO HAVE BY MY SIDE IN THE LONG TERM.

Adolescence is the stage where I get to know myself, who I want to be, and to begin to consider what kind of person I want to have by my side in the long term, without naming them yet, and avoiding being distracted by physical attraction.

📖 FOCUS ON TRUTH

Having feelings for someone is not the same as loving someone. The Word of God is very clear regarding love in all its dimensions. We will analyze in this section two aspects of love: the love of God and human love.

There are many passages that define the love of God. We will study just one of them:

> *And I pray that you, being rooted and established in love,*
> *may have power, together with all the Lord's holy people, to grasp how*
> *wide and long and high and deep is the love of Christ, and to know this*
> *love that surpasses knowledge—that you may be filled to*
> *the measure of all the fullness of God.*

Ephesians 3:17–19

God loves all humanity and all his creation. His love is infinite, and it is not exclusive to only a few. Everyone can access it. However, the passage says that for those who have put their faith in Christ, He comes to dwell in their hearts, so that in this way they can take root and be grounded in love.

Verse 17 explains this to us with two images that resemble the love of God. The first is the roots, which is what supports a tree. If the roots are deeper, the love will be higher and stronger. The second image is that of the foundations, which is a construction word. It leads us to know that our life must be built on the basis of God's love in us. The two images tell us that love is the first thing, the basic thing, the essential thing to know God. Once that happens, each child of God can experience the different dimensions of God's love. Then verses 18 and 19 tell us about four dimensions: width, length, height, and depth. It could look like this:

The love of God is...

...so wide that it covers all of humanity and the entire creation.

...so long that it accompanies us throughout the entire journey of our lives.

...so high that it connects us with heaven itself.

...so deep that it knows the most intimate parts of us.

IF GOD IS LOVE, AND WE ARE HIS CHILDREN, WE MUST IMITATE HIM IN EVERYTHING, SEEKING TO BE LIKE HIM.

Width is the dimension that makes us look to the sides, to the left and to the right, that is, to others, to those around us. The love we receive from God must be poured out on others.

Length is the dimension that makes us look forward. God's love gives us a complete and clear vision of our paths, and creates for us a goal to follow, which is Christ himself.

Height makes us look up to the sky, which is where God moves, because he is love. Every perfect gift comes from above, from the Father, so that everything we are and all we have is from God and for God.

Depth makes us look inside ourselves at our condition and evaluate what should not be there. God's deep love forgives us of all sin and gives us freedom despite our past.

Now, let's talk a little about human love:

Follow God's example, therefore, as dearly loved children and walk in the way of love, just as Christ loved us and gave himself up for us as a fragrant offering and sacrifice to God.

But among you there must not be even a hint of sexual immorality, or of any kind of impurity, or of greed, because these are improper for God's holy people.

Ephesians 5:1–3

What teachings does this verse leave us?

First teaching: Let us imitate God because we are his beloved children. If God is love, and we are his children, we must imitate him in everything, seeking to be like him. If Christ loved us, we must walk as he walked:

Whoever claims to live in him must live as Jesus did.

1 John 2:6

Second teaching: Let us live loving others by the example of Christ. Our surrender to love others is a sacrifice that produces a pleasing perfume to God. It is a great offering that we can dedicate to him. Furthermore, this is how others will know that we are disciples of Christ:

By this everyone will know that you are my disciples, if you love one another.

John 13:35

Third teaching: Let us totally avoid sexual sins, impurity, and greed, because they are selfish ways of perverting the genuine love that we have received from God.

Love does not commit sin against others, because it is long-suffering, kind, does not seek its own, and keeps no record of wrongs:

> Love is patient, love is kind. It does not envy, it does not boast, it is not proud. It does not dishonor others, it is not self-seeking, it is not easily angered, it keeps no record of wrongs.
>
> **1 Corinthians 13:4–5**

As you can see, love is not subject to sentimental relationships. It is a culture, a way of thinking and acting. It is the essence of God in us, because God is love.

There is nothing greater than the love of God manifested by his children!

INTROSPECTION

A key thought-provoking question to ask teenagers is: What does it take to be ready for a relationship? Here are some possible answers:

- Long-term commitment. If someone is uninterested in engaging in courtship with the expectation of marriage, this would indicate that the person does not value the relationship or doesn't value marriage.

- Independence to make decisions. If you are of an age where your parents already allow you to make your own decisions, you have a point in your favor. If you are not that age, then it is not the time yet.

- Emotional maturity. You cannot start a relationship if one day you love that person and the next day you want to end the relationship.

- Self-control. If you are not able to contain your sexual urges, you are not yet in a position to maintain a healthy courtship.

- Selfishness. A relationship involves thinking about the other, and nor-mally a teenager is focused on himself most of the time. Knowing that you should care about the other person is an essential requirement for anyone who wants to have a dating relationship.

- Have a clear purpose. The relationship of a couple has a purpose from heaven. If you don't understand the natural and spiritual purpose of a relationship, then you're not ready for one yet.

Now that we're on the subject of purpose, it might be a good idea to share with your group the need for everything we do to have a clear, focused, God-given purpose. Without this, nothing on earth makes sense. The mature purpose of a relationship is never to satisfy appearances, or because everyone is doing it, or because I'm the only one without a boyfriend or girlfriend, or just because I like someone. While not every relationship will end in a wedding, we do need to teach teens that they can't waste time or waste their emotions on just anyone. Purpose-less relationships are often short, focused on satisfaction, physically and emotionally unstable, and cause unnecessary wounds in the soul of teenagers. That is why it is better to avoid them until we can see God's holy purpose for the relationship which is the complete love of marriage and the beginning of a family.

 REFLECT ON A CHARACTER

CAMILO AND EVALUNA

Being a teen with healthy values and working in the artistic world is a huge challenge, and even more so when you have had an encounter with Jesus and decide to lead a life within God's parameters. When fame reaches a Christian teenager, their faith is put to the test. The cloud of witnesses has a very high expectation, and many are led to want to meet it. They become idols, gain cult status, and people expect them to behave as an artist should.

Camilo grew up with talent to spare. God opened unimaginable doors for him with artists who wanted to sing his songs, but the boy who wrote youthful and catchy lyrics also wanted to try his hand at being a singer. Since his adolescence, Camilo naturally expressed his decision to proclaim the blessings of Christ on his life and the way in which God had given him direction and hope.

Evaluna was born in a Christian home and in the shadow of her famous father Ricardo Montaner, who also trained her in the world of music. Her first song, titled *La gloria de Dios* (The Glory of God) was recorded with him, and is an expression of her faith and conviction.

Camilo and Evaluna started dating and pretty soon decided to get engaged and unite in marriage, and from what could be seen in the media, they were not part of any scandal but handled it very normally.

QUESTIONS FOR THE DISCIPLES

- Is it easy to have a healthy and exemplary courtship today? Why or why not?

- In what ways can society try to divert us from doing things according to God's purposes? What can we do to protect ourselves from this?

ISAAC AND REBEKAH

The story of this couple is found in the book of Genesis. You can read the beginning of this story in chapter 24, and from there we can discern some very important values for a romantic relationship. Abraham did not want his son to marry just anyone. That is why he sent his servant to look for a wife fir his son from among his relatives. This is a warning to us of what being unequally yoked represents. A person with other beliefs, with a different attitude toward God, with other cultural values, will always bring conflict to the relationship.

Abraham's servant asked God for several tests to find out if the chosen person was the right one. When we direct a teenager in the sentimental areas of life, we must teach them to verify God's will in the midst of their choices. Depending on the culture and family convictions, the age at which teenagers are allowed to start a relationship is different. However, it is good that as a discipler you can prepare your boys and girls so that, when the time comes, as it will sooner or later, they can make the best decisions.

In Genesis 24:58 we see how Rebekah's brother and mother left the decision to go with Abraham's servant in the young lady's hands: "*So they called Rebekah and asked her, 'Will you go with this man? 'I will go,' she said."*

According to the culture of that time, the servant and the maiden's relatives could have made the decision without consulting her, but they decided not to, and Rebekah was able to make this decision wisely. The takeaway here is that the maiden being discipled must learn both to say yes and to say no.

For his part, Abraham's servant was certain that this woman was the one chosen by God to be Isaac's wife because of all the tests and confirmations that he had asked the Lord for. The takeaway here is that as you prepare your teens for the day they might be in a relationship, you need to help them see beyond the emotions of the moment.

QUESTIONS FOR THE DISCIPLES:

- What do you dream that your relationship as a couple will be?

- What do you think is the best way to decide who is the right person?

MOBILIZE

The great achievement of this lesson in the discipleship project for teenagers is not that they end up with good information, but that they make some important commitments:

- The first is to decide to subject their loving plans to the lordship of Christ, that is to say that whatever they dream of and desire will be connected with God's desires and premises.

- The second is to decide to subject their feelings of love to the lordship of Christ, because it is one thing to have the right plans and another to manage their feelings intelligently.

- The third is to commit to waiting on their feelings and plans for love until the right moment, after they finish their studies and define their identity. Your teenagers should understand that even though they feel attracted to someone does not mean that it is time to start a loving relationship; this will protect them from making many bad decisions. Help them get deadlines and expectations right by going back to the first commitment on this list.

And finally, it would be good to convey to your teenagers that the highest rate of success in relationships is in those that have close spiritual accompaniment. If you lack someone to accompany you in these processes, you run the risk of making many mistakes.

LESSON 8

HEALTHY RELATIONSHIPS

The story we find in the Bible is that of a being who loves and continues to love even when it is not reciprocated.

Itiel Arroyo, *Love is For The Brave*

One of the most popular TV shows of all time has been *Friends.*

The series was a hit in the 90s and has continued in popularity until today. For many people the three female leads and the three male leads created what people imagined an ideal friendship is. What happened in each episode was a reflection of the culture of that decade in the United States. However, the dynamics between them meant that the series did not lose relevance. This is true because friendship will always be an important issue for everyone, as we all share the need to have good friend.

🧠 AVALANCHE OF IDEAS

Write each of the following on separate pieces of paper:

- Dad

- Mom

- Grandparents

- Older siblings

- Younger siblings

- Uncles/Aunts

- Cousins

- Best friend

- Other friends

- Classmates

- Neighbors

- Social media friends

- Friends from church

- Leaders or mentors

Place all the papers randomly on a table or use masking tape behind them to stick them on a board. If you're in a virtual meeting, have the words appear on the screen. Then ask the group to rank these people according to their importance, but to do it as a group, that is, not for each one to say their own order, but for them to talk among themselves and argue until there is a consensus, while you watch them.

After they have agreed and finished with their ideal list, tell them to pretend to be children and decide again what order they would assign to each person from that perspective. Finally, have them rank the people as if they were an elderly person.

NOW HELP THEM TO CONTINUE REFLECTING

- What changes occurred in each case when the perspective changed?

- At what stage are friends most important and why?

- What relationships are less common but very important?

 FOUNDATIONS OF THE THEME

One of the great challenges during adolescence is the proper and wise management of friendships. Every relationship is like a building that is built as tall as one wants. However, to continue building, sometimes we must remove the rubble that has been left over from incidents that have occurred within that relationship. We all go through conflicts, disappointments, and betrayals and if we are honest, we are just as responsible for these evils as others. The point is that among imperfect people relationships are never perfect, but that's no excuse for not being intentional about working on them, and teens may just start doing that at this stage. We all need support, appreciation, and confidence, and we can all give them.

ONE OF THE GREAT CHALLENGES DURING ADOLESCENCE IS THE PROPER AND WISE MANAGEMENT OF FRIENDSHIPS.

The inner being of teenagers is continually screaming:

- I need you to know me and value me!

- I need you to listen and understand me!

- I need you to know who I am and why I act like this!

- I need you not to compare me with others!

- I need you to take the time to see my heart!

For this reason, we, the adults, the parents, the leaders, the disciplers, need to be wise in the way we help them build their network of relationships, especially teaching them principles so that they can take care of their relationships when we aren't there.

A serious mistake by parents, for example, would be to settle for just supporting the home financially and dedicating the rest of the time to their own concerns rather than being intentional about establishing a healthy and strong relationship with their children as they grow up. If this is common in childhood, it is very likely that their relationship with their children will suffer when adolescence arrives, and then it will be an uphill battle trying to make up for lost time. For leaders and disciplers the challenge is similar. If we only focus on holding meetings and don't develop a relationship with our disciples, their spiritual life may revolve around the meeting, but they will end up just meeting an attendance requirement, and creating their real lives with those with whom they have more intimate relationships. If they fail to see us as confidants, advisers, mentors, and older siblings, then they are too far away for us to also be role models and a positive influence in their lives.

AMONG IMPERFECT PEOPLE RELATIONSHIPS ARE NEVER PERFECT.

Pastor Héctor Hermosillo writes in the book *Pastorea a tu hijo adolescente* (Pastor Your Adolescent Child):

"The best teacher in the world established and modeled himself what, after much research, educators have recognized as the ideal vehicle to transmit any knowledge: LOVE."

📖 FOCUS ON TRUTH

The Bible is a relational book. Read this passage with them:

One who has unreliable friends soon comes to ruin,
but there is a friend who sticks closer than a brother.

Proverbs 18:24

This verse shows us two extremes of what a friendship can be. There are certain friendships that at one point in life can be toxic. For one reason or another they can cause headaches and bad decisions. On the other hand, there are friends we can count on unconditionally; we know that we can trust them because of their faithfulness and transparency with us.

This makes us see the importance of choosing our friends well.

Does that mean that if you have toxic friendships, you should stay away from them?

THE BIBLE IS A RELATIONAL BOOK.

Probably so, at least during a certain stage (like adolescence) or perhaps at specific time periods (like a school year, or even a camp or event). If friendship with a person is synonymous with bad decisions, then your best decision with that person might be to separate from them.

Look at these other verses:

Perfume and incense bring joy to the heart,
and the pleasantness of a friend springs from their heartfelt advice. Do
not forsake your friend or a friend of your family,
and do not go to your relative's house when disaster strikes you—
better a neighbor nearby than a relative far away.

Proverbs 27:9–10

This passage is powerful because it brings together several notions regarding friendship. First, it describes the personal satisfaction that comes from having a friend you can trust and ask for advice. Then, it mentions the urgency of being faithful so as not to abandon a friend, not even our father's friend! This tells us about the deep appreciation that we should give to friendship, but also to the family. Finally, it compares friendship with brotherhood, and touches on the subject of people who are close to us, like a neighbor, who can sometimes become as close as a brother if we know that we can always count on that person. By analyzing all these points, it is easy to understand how important it is for a disciple to choose their friends and the people around them well!

The following passage talks about fellow soldiers:

I long to see you so that I may impart to you some spiritual gift to make you strong—that is, that you and I may be mutually encouraged by each other's faith.

Romans 1:11–12

Here Paul is speaking to the church in Rome, highlighting what a blessing it is to feel encouraged by one another. It is very important to have good friends who accompany us in our process as disciples. From them we will receive an impartation of the Spirit of God, and we will also feed on what God has spoken to them. We must also reciprocate with them: support them, pray for them, accompany them when they are going through difficult situations, and not leave them alone. They are another important type of friend!

Scripture also mentions several principles, which we could call "One Another Principles":

- Help one another. (Hebrews 10:24)

- Live in harmony with one another. (Romans 12:16)

- Love one another. (1 John 4:11)

- Encourage and edify one another. (1 Thessalonians 5:11)

- Carry one another's burdens. (Galatians 6:2)

- Stop criticizing one another. (Romans 14:13)

- Support and forgive one another. (Colossians 3:13–15)

These instructions guide us to think about the neighbor who is close to us.

Now let's talk about the relationship with our parents. This relationship is based on honor:

"Honor your father and mother," and "love your neighbor as yourself."

Matthew 19:19

Jesus, speaking with the rich young man, answers several things regarding the intention of fulfilling the law. Among these things, Jesus mentions two important aspects related to relationships with the people close to us. On the one hand, he talks about honoring parents. This was a principle handed down from generation to generation since ancient times. It was part of their culture, their lifestyle. There was no way to think of living a life that dishonored parents. God's ideal is that we have a very close relationship with them!

> **JESUS'S WORDS WERE POWERFUL, NOT BECAUSE THEY HAD FANCY REVELATIONS BUT BECAUSE HE SPOKE TRUTHS OF LIFE.**

On the other hand, Jesus also spoke of loving our neighbor, someone close to us, a friend, and included this condition: we must do it with the same sincerity with which we love ourselves. Jesus's words were powerful, not because they had fancy revelations but because he spoke truths of life.

How do you receive these passages of Scripture? How could your life change after reading them?

INTROSPECTION

A good process for establishing healthy relationships revolves around these four ideas:

1. **Zero Hypocrisy.** One of the best attributes a person can bring to a healthy relationship is integrity. Integrity is closely related to honesty, openness, the desire to be genuine, and acting without hypocrisy. A relationship that is filled with lies, falsehood, deceit, and suspicion cannot be built in a healthy way.

2. **Show empathy.** This idea of putting yourself in the other's shoes in order to understand them was not invented by any philosopher. God

invented it, and it's called mercy. It is the ability to grieve with the pain of another, to help them carry their burdens, to suffer together, and to rejoice in their successes. It's nice to have someone like that walking with us!

3. **Develop familiarity.** How close we consider a person has to do with the time we have invested in being together. Quantity of time and quality of time too. It's not about going to live with someone, or spending all day at their house and even sleeping there (although sometimes it happens!), but it does have to do with taking advantage of the valuable moments that life offers to share them with someone else.

4. **Establish links.** When a relationship is built well, without hypocrisy, showing empathy, and developing familiarity, it is time to establish links. By this we mean finding those things by which you join in a more personal and close way with the other person.

Share these ideas with the group and then the questions stage begins... that's the best part!

Which of these principles do your friends already meet?

Think about relationships you've had in the past that have broken up. Which of these principles were broken?

Have you valued these principles when choosing friends in the past? Which ones yes, and which ones no? How did those relationships turn out?

If there is a broken relationship that you want to recover, do you think it is possible? Why or why not?

REFLECT ON A CHARACTER

HAN SOLO AND CHEWBACCA, AND R2D2 AND C-3PO

The *Star Wars* universe presents several examples of lasting friendship. Two of the best-known friend duos are Han Solo and Chewbacca, and the droids R2D2 and C-3PO.

Both in the case of the pilots of the Millennium Falcon and of the droids that intertwine practically throughout the entire saga, one of them always understands the language of the other without us, as the audience, being able to understand them. We hear the furry friend make animal noises, and we hear the smallest droid make beeping sounds, however their friends understand them perfectly and perhaps that is the great secret of their friendship.

QUESTIONS FOR THE DISCIPLES

- How can we make friends with people we don't even need to use words with to communicate?

- For personal evaluation: do you have friends like Han Solo or C-3PO? What should you do to have friends like that?

DAVID AND JONATHAN

The Bible records the friendship between Saul's son Jonathan and David, the king who had been anointed to take the throne shortly. Saul had become uncomfortable with David. When the people acclaimed the young warrior, the king wanted to hang him. Slowly, Saul's discomfort turned into inordinate jealousy, and later he began a terrible persecution against David, whom he thought was a stubborn adversary who wanted to take his throne.

David built a valuable friendship with Saul's son Jonathan. Jonathan became someone very important in his life, and that was key at that moment, since the conflict was not temporary but became a kind of civil war, with some supporting David and others (especially the royal army) Saul. By then, Jonathan promised to be David's informant in order to protect him from his father.

What a hard situation! Imagine how strong their friendship was, that Jonathan preferred to turn against his father, the king, to be on the side of his friend. David, in the same way, had to trust Jonathan even though he was the son of his persecutor, and he was able to do so because he trusted the friendship that both had built.

QUESTION FOR THE DISCIPLES

- How do you think David and Jonathan came to have such a trusting relationship?

 MOBILIZE

Choose three of the "One Another Principles" we learned about in the Focus on Truth portion and challenge your disciples to practice them throughout the week, knowing that they will have to share their experience during the next meeting. Make sure the chosen actions are specific. Ideally, have them choose them out loud in front of the others.

By the end of the week, you will see that those who did it will speak enthusiastically and feel better about themselves. That should be highlighted when they finish talking, to affirm the actions, and then have them repeat the exercise, especially to give those who haven't done as much a chance to do more.

LESSON 9

SPIRITUAL NARCISSISM

*It is not love that should be depicted as blind,
but self-love.*

Voltaire

According to Greek mythology, Narcissus was a very handsome young man whose life revolved around himself, considering himself superior to others. He is the origin of the term "narcissism." A dictionary would define "narcissism" as an excessive admiration that a person feels for themselves, for their physical appearance, or for their gifts or qualities. If we join this concept with the word "spiritual," this indicates someone who believes that God is there to serve them, because everything in the Christian life or in the ministry is about what they do.

A basic aspect of a spiritual narcissist comes to light in their prayers, since they only focus on their own needs, desires, and tastes, and their vision lacks a sense of group or community. A spiritual narcissist doesn't think about what they can do for God, but what God can do for them. In addition, they do not make an effort to live according to the perfect will of the Father, because they have believed in a misleading gospel that tells them that God is there to fulfill their aspirations.

Everyone at some point in our Christian life can go through stages of spiritual narcissism: questioning God for not getting what we want, for not helping us, or not granting us what we asked for. We end up turning God, the King of the universe, into our "special spiritual delivery," which must deliver to us as soon as possible any request that we make. Clearly, this behavior of a spiritual narcissist is a sign of immaturity, and we need to help our teens move past this brand of Christianity.

AVALANCHE OF IDEAS

After the introduction, invite your teens to put together a list of the top ten characteristics of a spiritual narcissist. You can stop at each one for as long as you want to explain them, and then rank them.

Some of the characteristics that you can suggest if they have trouble identifying them are the following:

- They pray every morning that everything goes well for them and that everything goes according to what they have planned.

- Thay complain to God about what they have asked for and have not received.

- They do not ask for others, since they cannot see the needs of others.

- They think that others should serve them, open the door for them, sing to help them worship, preach the Word, etc.

- They don't serve because they don't have time; their schedule is filled with many things that take them away from service in any form.

- Some spiritual narcissists choose to serve, but they do so to get something in return, such as recognition or admiration.

- They never focus on what God asks them to do but rather on what they ask God to do.

Ask about other examples and what they think about these characteristics.

 FOUNDATIONS OF THE THEME

The true gospel has much more to do with giving than receiving. It requires giving up things, rather than asking for them. It implies dying to oneself in order to rise again. If you look closely, the gospel of the kingdom of heaven that Christ preached and lived is the exact opposite of what the world commonly seeks. Christ taught that to win you have to lose, to live you have to die, and to enter the kingdom you don't have to be great and powerful but you have to be like children. He also said that the last will be the first, and that to be a leader you must first be the one who serves everyone.

THE GOSPEL OF THE KINGDOM OF HEAVEN THAT CHRIST PREACHED AND LIVED IS THE EXACT OPPOSITE OF WHAT THE WORLD COMMMONLY SEEKS.

The gospel was not designed to give us our passing whims and desires, although that occasionally happens. So, God's idea is not that we go looking for him in order to receive his favors, or that we behave like good children to have the right to receive everything we ask for. In contrast to the list we used earlier to describe a spiritual narcissist, the following is a list of attitudes that the Bible teaches to be correct.

Disciples of Christ:

- Pray that God's will would be accomplished in and through their life.

- Acknowledge God's sovereignty when they don't receive something they asked for.

- Are used to asking for others, praying for those in need, and even blessing those who have wronged them.

- Forgive those who have offended them and do not curse.

- Are convinced that the best way to love God is by serving others.

- Remain humble, even if they have reached high level rank or positions, and do not aim for recognition and admiration.

- Always ask God before making decisions, and submit to his perfect will manifested in his Word.

As long as our decisions are focused on satisfying our own desires, we will be spiritual narcissists. If we want to stop being one, we must understand that the Christian life is not about how many favors we receive from God, but about how willing we are to lead a life according to his will.

📖 FOCUS ON TRUTH

Let's delve into this biblical passage together:

To some who were confident of their own righteousness and looked down on everyone else, Jesus told this parable: "Two men went up to the temple to pray, one a Pharisee and the other a tax collector. The Pharisee stood by himself and prayed: 'God, I thank you that I am not like other people—robbers, evildoers, adulterers—or even like this tax collector. I fast twice a week and give a tenth of all I get.'

"But the tax collector stood at a distance. He would not even look up to heaven, but beat his breast and said, 'God, have mercy on me, a sinner.'

"I tell you that this man, rather than the other, went home justified before God. For all those who exalt themselves will be humbled, and those who humble themselves will be exalted."

Luke 18:9–14

When Jesus told this story, he described very well the attitude of a spiritual narcissist with the example of the Pharisee. For this person, giving thanks had to do with putting others down and feeling superior, particularly pointing fingers at the tax collector. It must be considered that at that time tax collectors were frowned upon among the people of Israel, since their work was in favor of the Roman

Empire. The taxes they collected impoverished their Hebrew brothers and enriched Rome. Thus, the contrast between these two people was vast.

The Pharisee, who should have been the person most aware of who God is and therefore should have walked in humility, lifted himself up! He considered himself to be better than others, judged them, and thought that fasting, tithing, and keeping certain aspects of the law were enough to stand right before God and make him worthy of admiration. He never considered the attitude of his heart. Certainly, this man was a spiritual narcissist!

ONE PERSON MAY KEEP MANY ASPECTS OF GOD'S LAW FOR THE WRONG REASONS.

By contrast, the tax collector was hated by his own people and despised by the Romans. But he was sure of his condition as a sinner, to the point of not being able to even raise his eyes to heaven because he felt unworthy of the Father's favor.

For the people who heard this allegory from the mouth of Jesus, it must have been a shock. Jesus spoke well of someone they judged to be evil, and he spoke ill of someone they considered a spiritual authority. However, Jesus's intention was not to confuse people but to teach them to see beyond appearances. One person may keep many aspects of God's law for the wrong reasons, while another may have the right attitude in his heart even though others judge him to be unrighteous.

Jesus presents here a spiritual principle that is inexorably fulfilled. He who exalts himself will at some point be humbled, while he who acknowledges his condition as a sinner and humbles himself before God, will be exalted in due time.

Now let's look at the following passage:

Do nothing out of selfish ambition or vain conceit. Rather, in humility value others above yourselves, not looking to your own interests but each of you to the interests of the others.

In your relationships with one another, have the same mindset as Christ Jesus.

Philippians 2:3–5

In this case, Paul recommends to the Philippians that they be attentive to this kind of attitude. Pride, arrogance, and haughtiness are the kind of attitudes that cannot be easily seen in oneself. Recognizing that we are living out of self-ishness or vanity is not an easy thing! Pride is a subtle and accurate weapon of the enemy, who seeks to make us believe that we are better than others. Paul's instruction on this is clear: we should not seek only our own good, but seek the good of others. Let us watch the intentions of our hearts at every moment!

Let's continue reading the following verses:

Who, being in very nature God,
did not consider equality with God something to be used to his own advan-tage; rather, he made himself nothing by taking the very nature of a ser-vant, being made in human likeness. And being found in appearance as a man, he humbled himself by becoming obedient to death—
even death on a cross!

Therefore God exalted him to the highest place
and gave him the name that is above every name, that at the name of Jesus every knee should bow,
in heaven and on earth and under the earth, and every tongue acknowl-edge that Jesus Christ is Lord,
to the glory of God the Father.

Philippians 2:6–11

Look at the humility of Jesus:

- He didn't cling to the fact that he was God, but he stripped himself of that condition to reach us.

- He took the form of a servant, making himself like men.

- As a man, he humbled himself to give himself up for us.

- By turning himself in, he decided to voluntarily accept death, and not just any death but the cruelest and most shameful way of dying at the time.

- For all this, the Father decided to exalt him, giving him a name superior to all names.

- For this reason also, before the name of Jesus every knee shall bow, and every tongue shall confess that he is Lord, to the glory of God the Father.

The story of Jesus is not that of someone who becomes great after being small, a nobody who becomes powerful, or someone who prospers after being poor. His story is the opposite. He is the one who, having everything, decided to leave it to serve.

⚙ INTROSPECTION

Reread the passage from Luke 18:9-14 together.

On one side are the attitudes of the Pharisee, who boasts of his knowledge, his unequivocal compliance with the law, his social status, and his leadership position. On the other side are the attitudes of the publican, such as humility, submission before God, and the recognition of his status as a sinner and his consequent need to be forgiven.

YOU CAN ASK YOUR DISCIPLES THESE QUESTIONS

- Which of these two characters do you identify with the most, and why?

- If you had to put your own life on a scale, which side would you lean more toward?

- What traits of a spiritual narcissist do you recognize in yourself?

- What character flaws or attitudes should you give up to tip the scales to the right side?

Finally, help your disciples to develop a plan that allows them to maintain an attitude of constant renewal of mind, that makes them aware of their own need for Christ, and that transmits to them the urgent passion to fulfill his mission on earth.

Thinking of others before oneself says a lot about a true disciple of Christ.

 REFLECT ON A CHARACTER

LADY GAGA

Stefani Joanne Angelina Germanotta, better known by her stage name Lady Gaga, was born in 1986 and this millennial artist rose to fame when she was discovered by a record label, leaving her art studies at the age of nineteen to focus on her music career.

Stefani created Lady Gaga as an uninhibited and controversial character to draw attention to her art. She decided to explore the field of music, dance, fashion, and whatever activity was convenient. Her musical themes, choreographies, and videos have always aimed to highlight sexuality, sexual violence, and the body, and while no one can argue with her talent, it is obvious that the character had to go to some extremes to make that talent more valued or at least recognized.

Some will say that for a world-class artist it is necessary to behave in this way, but let's ask some questions in order to discuss the theme of this chapter.

QUESTIONS FOR THE DISCIPLES

- Why do many artists like Lady Gaga exaggerate with their outfits?

- How is fame or talent related to the need to be seen by others?

- Do you also feel the need for others to see you? How is this need evident in your life?

PAUL

Saul of Tarsus was a scholar of Scripture and considered the followers of Jesus to be rebellious and heretics for giving any man the title of Son of God. For this reason, he had become one of the biggest persecutors of the first believers in this Messiah, who had come to revolutionize tradition.

In his story, described in the book of Acts, it is said that at a certain moment Saul had a supernatural encounter with Jesus. From there, his name changed to Paul, and he became the apostle to the Gentiles, with a calling to preach the truth of Jesus Christ to all nations.

In his letter to the Philippians, chapter three, Paul describes his narcissistic condition before knowing Christ as Savior. He says that he valued his Hebrew lineage as a descendant of the tribe of Benjamin and valued his studies as a Pharisee at the feet of Gamaliel, and his status as a zealous adherent of God's law and blameless in his way of living. However, upon meeting Jesus, his perspective on life changed completely. Paul decided to throw away everything that previously made him feel superior to others, because he understood that the knowledge of Christ invaded him and prompted him to change his way of thinking and acting.

His change of mind was so radical that he later said things like:

Follow my example, as I follow the example of Christ.

1 Corinthians 11:1

A statement of this nature, acknowledging that now his life would be futile without Jesus, shows that Paul was a different person than before. Saul shed his status as a spiritual narcissist to become Paul, a true disciple of Jesus, humble and submissive to the will of God. His life no longer revolved around himself, but his spirit, soul, and body were now subjected to obeying the will of God, desperately seeking those who were lost.

QUESTIONS FOR THE DISCIPLES

- Do you identify with Paul in any aspect of your life?

- Do you think Paul's testimony is a good model for us? In what sense?

 # MOBILIZE

The objective of this lesson is to help our teenage disciples to look at the needs of others, including their approach to God.

The only way to get rid of spiritual narcissism is to put God first. Whem we do, we inevitably think of others. Discuss with your discipleship group some challenges in serving others. It is better if the decision of what to do comes from them. As a discipler, you can shape the discussion, but let the initiative come from the teens.

SOME IDEAS

- **A social work trip.** Visit a nursing home, an orphanage, centers for young people with different problems, or other social work entities. These types of activities will help your young people to develop social sensitivity and a burden for those who suffer the most. After a first visit, some of your young people may want to commit to providing more regular help to one of these institutions.

- **A family day.** Find a family that is going through an economic crisis. It can be from the same congregation that you attend (giving priority to the family of faith), although it can also be someone who is not a believer. Take food offerings or think of other needs that could be met for this family through this initiative.

- **Recycling campaigns.** Thinking about the environment can help some to stop thinking about their own condition and motivate them to take care of the planet. By doing this, we are changing the culture that surrounds us. This is not just a campaign, but it should become a new lifestyle. That is managing well what God gave us to take care of!

- **Support for animal shelters.** Sites that house stray dogs or cats often need a lot of help, and your teenagers can get in there, collaborating by bringing toys or other objects or donating a few hours to help the people who work there.

- **Personal burdens.** You can ask your young people to think of someone for whom they feel a special burden; someone they're worried about because they're going through a difficult situation, or just someone they'd like to see better. Encourage your young people to set aside time each week, or every other week, to spend time with this person and help them with whatever they need. This can also be the kickoff for these disciples to start discipling others!

There are many ways to think of others, and perhaps you can think of more ideas to add to this list. The important thing is that your teenagers understand the value of serving others.

Our faith becomes much more relevant and enjoyable when we leave behind the immaturity of spiritual narcissism and live with a continuous attitude of service to others. Overcoming that constant tendency to think of oneself can be difficult, but it is what we learn from Jesus.

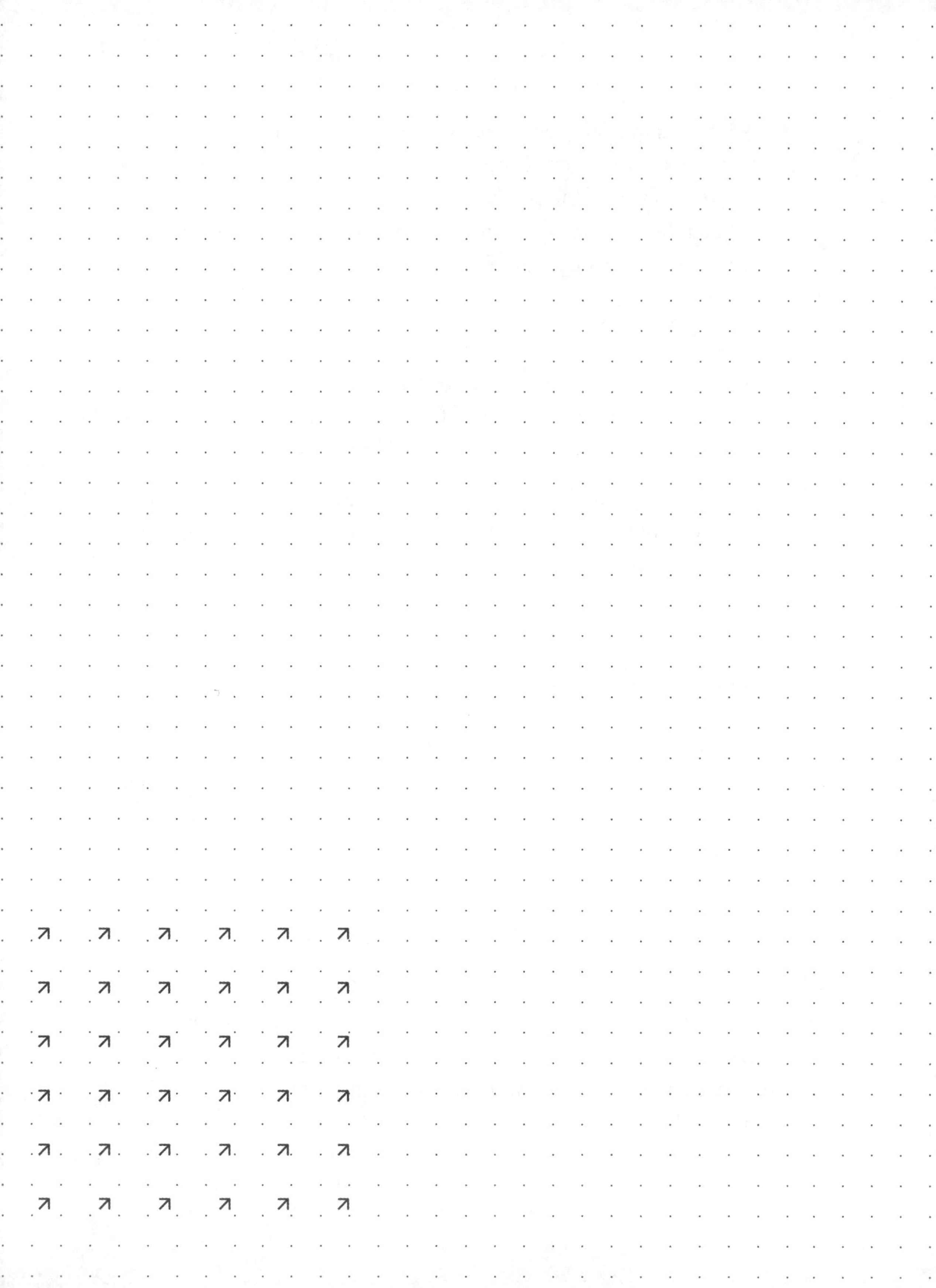

LESSON 10

BOUNDARIES AND FREEDOM

The desire of teenagers to become independent is not only normal but desirable.

John Townsend, *Boundaries with Teens*

A few years ago, the science fiction film *Limitless* was released, starring Bradley Cooper, Abbie Cornish, and Robert De Niro. In it, the magic of cinema takes us to a postmodern world where a nobody writer, due to those random coincidences in life, has the opportunity to take a pill that multiplies his brain capacity to the maximum. Because of this, the protagonist becomes capable of having all the information of his brain at his fingertips, and taking advantage of all his cognitive potential.

Imagine being able to organize your mind with everything you have learned, what your brain has recorded, the information you forgot, the books you read, the people you met, and you could memorize everything from short quotes from famous authors to entire books of all kinds. And what if this pill could teach you a language in days, or if you could learn to play an instrument in minutes? You could also investigate the most successful financial strategies in a few hours.

The film's plot first highlights the enormous possibilities that this pill represents, but then it takes a turn when the protagonist realizes that there are other characters looking for it too. His life is now at risk...

AVALANCHE OF IDEAS

Let's pretend that your group of disciples have taken those pills. Each of them is about to acquire extreme brain power. Make a list of abilities that you have invented and ask the group to choose the one that is closest to the personal interests of each one. It should not be each boy or girl who chooses, but the group must agree and assign each one the ability that the majority believes that the other should have.

Remember that you will need as many extreme ability options as there are people in the group. If there are too many, you can consider splitting the group in two, or repeating some of the abilities on two people.

Here are some ideas:

1. Ability to make money with business strategies

2. Ability to understand and speak any language in a few minutes

3. Ability to know what others are thinking

4. Ability to convince others to do what you want

5. Ability to read a book in a second

6. Ability to understand all the sciences of the world

7. Ability to predict the future

8. Ability to use technology to its fullest

9. Ability to dominate animals at will

10. Ability to prevent natural disasters

Now explain to them that each ability has a danger or price. And that when using it they are aware that they, or someone else will lose something. Then ask them: Will they help the world, or will they be selfish?

This is a trick questions, and you will only ask them so that they show some kindness and decide to help the world and do good deeds with their extreme abilities. After they finish sharing their ideas, tell them what the consequences were for using their acquired powers.

Here is the list of consequences, in the same order as the abilities list:

1. For every dollar you earn, someone will have to lose that dollar.

2. Every time you use your power, someone will lose their ability to speak.

3. When you use your power, someone else will go crazy.

4. Every time you use your power, there will be a divorce.

5. For every book you read, someone will go blind.

6. Every time you learn a new science, a thousand schools will close.

7. When you use your power, someone will forget their past.

8. By using your power, the light of a city will be lost for a week.

9. When you use your ability, a species will become extinct.

10. By using your power, a new natural disaster will appear in another place.

Once your teens have brainstormed what they would do to help the world, you will reveal their weaknesses, or the consequences of using their extreme abilities. No one will like it, but that is precisely the purpose for which God has set limits for us that we should not exceed.

FOUNDATIONS OF THE THEME

Limits are neutral. There are some that are good and others that are unnecessary, and the strategy of life is to discern which are the ones God put in place to protect us.

That said, we can differentiate between the different types of limits that exist. Some are natural limits, created by God to govern nature itself. That is why it is logical that birds have the ability to fly and cows do not. Imagine a cow pooping in the air!

In addition to the limits in nature, God has established moral limits, limits on interpersonal relationships, limits on marriages, limits on sexuality, etc. Every aspect of life has been designed by God to fit into a space where we can all successfully fulfill our purpose without harming others, and instead be of benefit to others. In this sense, limits

LIMITS ARE BOUNDARIES THAT GOD HAS INTENTIONALLY PLACED TO MAINTAIN ORDER IN ALL THINGS.

are boundaries that God has intentionally placed to maintain order in all things. And yes, of course, also to keep the human being in order. Every time the human being has exceeded a limit, it has been to the detriment of someone else. Another ends up being damaged, offended, or affected in some way by what this person did. That's why limits are good.

And what about freedom?

Yes, God set us free too. However, that freedom we have must be bounded by certain parameters so that it does not get out of control. God's idea was not to establish a list of restrictions to have something to bother the human being with. Rather, limits are his way of helping us to manage our own lives wisely, without affecting others, in order to enjoy the benefits that we have as human beings.

Exceeding the limits of God generates slavery.

Crossing the limits breaks marriages, families are divided, friendships are lost, and people are hurt. By exceeding the limits, human beings are corrupted, and societies are broken, rulers become evil emperors and oppression increases, and that is why wars and world conflicts also come.

In fact, a good definition of sin is: exceeding the limits set by God.

174

That's why we need to have limits.

Limits define in our life, so that it does not get out of control. Being clear about the limits that I must respect as a child of God, and above all as a disciple of Jesus, gives me enough freedom to live according to God's will.

EXCEEDING THE LIMITS OF GOD GENERATES SLAVERY.

Putting definitive boundaries in my life makes me:

- Know who I am and how far I can go.

- Think of the other and not just myself.

- Know my responsibilities and enjoy my rights.

- Know how to distinguish between good and bad to choose well.

Adapted from the book *Boundaries* by Henry Cloud and John Townsend, Some problems that show the lack of limits are:

- Not being able to say no

- Wanting to please everyone

- Saying no to good things

- Not respecting the limits of others

- Not listening to others when they say no

- Wanting to control the decisions of others

- Manipulating situations through emotions

- Always wanting to get away with everything

When we examine our own lives and recognize that we still have personal boundaries to work on, we shouldn't procrastinate. It is an urgent need, and if we pay attention to it, we will lead successful lives and be at peace with people and with God.

What does this have to do with discipleship?

HAVING PROPER BOUNDARIES MEANS NOT GOING BEYOND WHERE GOD HAS TOLD YOU TO GO.

Well, everything. Your lifestyle and your decisions will depend a lot on the limits that you decide to respect, prioritizing the effect that your actions may have on others. It is not about repressing yourself or lacking personal desires. In the things you decide to pursue, there is no limit. You can reach the sky! Having proper boundaries means not going beyond where God has told you to go, especially if the result will harm other people.

That is why houses have boundaries that you cannot exceed. If someone enters yours without your permission, you will tell them that they are on private property. That is why no one canlegally enter a country without having registered at the border before they have crossed its boundary or limit. If you don't register, you will be an illegal person in that place.

Likewise, if someone wants to go beyond what they are allowed to go with you, you will tell them that they can't. No one can touch another improperly, as it would be exceeding a limit. No one should say harmful words to another, as that exceeds the limits we have put in place.

In every aspect of life, choosing to live in holiness is choosing to live attached to the limits that God has established.

📖 FOCUS ON TRUTH

Many uninformed people repeat that God's law is full of prohibitions that make us increasingly unhappy. In fact, many current ideologies and philosophical tendencies state that to be happy we must have fewer controls and more freedom, without realizing that this idea of freedom is the biggest enemy of human rights.

God did not create laws to put the human being in a prison. On the contrary, he gives the human being the opportunity to see through his eyes the consequences of doing this or that, and he has provided us with his advice to help us measure the consequences of our freedoms. That is what consciousness is all about.

The book of Genesis tells us that when God created the human being, he gave them specific instructions on what to do and what not to do. If only Adam and Eve had listened, we would have a world with greater freedom today. Yes, with true freedom! Unfortunately, they decided to disobey God's instructions and exceed the established limit, and to this day we suffer the consequences.

Let's read chapter 38 of the book of Job. It is really impressive! The text begins like this:

> *Then the* Lord *spoke to Job out of the storm. He said: "Who is this that obscures my plans with words without knowledge? Brace yourself like a man; I will question you, and you shall answer me.*
>
> *"Where were you when I laid the earth's foundation? Tell me, if you understand. Who marked off its dimensions? Surely you know! Who stretched a measuring line across it? On what were its footings set, or who laid its cornerstone while the morning stars sang together and all the angels shouted for joy?"*

Job 38:1–7

After waiting a while in silence, listening to the complaints and ravings of the pretentious Job, God decides to respond from the whirlwind by letting him know the difference between a mere mortal and the Creator of the universe, the one who laid the foundations of the Earth and calculated its dimensions, the one who gave it sustenance in endless space, while all the angels looked at his work in ecstasy.

Keep reading:

> *Who shut up the sea behind doors when it burst forth from the womb, when I made the clouds its garment and wrapped it in thick darkness, when I fixed limits for it and set its doors and bars in place, when I said, "This far you may come and no farther; here is where your proud waves halt"?*
>
> **Job 38:8–11**

It was God who set limits to the seas that grew proud from the depths; he enclosed them by establishing borders. And so he did with everything in creation, including the human being. Limits are healthy and they bring us freedom. Without limits we live at the expense of our own selfishness and evil.

What did Job learn?

- That God is sovereign and infinitely wise.

- That without its limits the world is chaos.

- That God gave us freedom to govern the earth, but not to exceed its limits.

- That sometimes we know so little about God, or are so arrogant, that we decide to defy his advice, but this always ends badly.

We see all this later, in chapter 42. There, Job reflects and summarizes what he has learned:

> Then Job replied to the Lord: "I know that you can do all things; no purpose of yours can be thwarted. You asked, 'Who is this that obscures my plans without knowledge?' *Surely I spoke of things I did not understand, things too wonderful for me to know.*

"You said, 'Listen now, and I will speak; I will question you, and you shall answer me.' My ears had heard of you but now my eyes have seen you. Therefore I despise myself and repent in dust and ashes."

Job 42:1–6

Job understood that everything he had said before when judging God was huge stupidity on his part. And finally, he understood that the limits that God established were the best for human beings. He says, "I had heard of you, but now my eyes have seen you." Job knew God more deeply through everything that happened to him. His eyes were opened, and he could see the magnificence of the Creator who set limits to the seas and designed everything with perfect intelligence. This revelation would forever change his destiny, just as it can change ours when we finally understand these things.

INTROSPECTION

Allow the group to consider various situations where nature has gotten out of hand. You can give them some ideas such as tsunamis, earthquakes, tidal waves, fires, floods, droughts, etc.

And what happens when human beings exceed their boundaries?

Here you can discuss various types of boundaries that every teen should consider.

What boundaries should I put on

- ...the way I dress?

- ...the way I speak?

- ...the things I see on the internet?

- ...the time I spend playing video games?

- ...how I approach the opposite sex?

- ...the way I respect and honor my parents?

- ...what I eat?

You can add as many ideas to this list as you like, considering the particular needs of your group of disciples and what you have seen in them. This is a good opportunity to help them recognize the ways they have overstepped boundaries, and to correct them with love!

 REFLECT ON A CHARACTER

MILEY CYRUS

Miley Cyrus was a little girl who became known thanks to her performance in the Disney Channel children's series, Hannah Montana. From that success, her career began to explode as a singer as well; she recorded several albums and even a movie. All when she was barely thirteen years old. As she then transitioned out of adolescence and left behind her childhood character, for many it was like watching her become an adult overnight.

Her performances became filled with uninhibited clothing and subject matter, and it didn't take long for her to be nude and start having sex and problems with drugs.

Many people lamented seeing the little girl who had been a positive influence on so many children because of the Disney series become her own antithesis in just a few years. She then came out as pansexual, got a divorce, and began openly supporting causes that produce more pain than freedom.

QUESTION FOR THE DISCIPLES

- What happened to Miley? She lost her limits. Success stole her childhood, and then she allowed her youth to be stolen from her.

DAVID

David's story is one of the most famous and well known of all time. The Bible has been in charge of describing its most glorious moments and its darkest as well. But what can we learn from David about limits?

A lot!

In the first book of the prophet Samuel the story of him is told, and you can really learn a lot from him if you read Scripture little by little. At the time when Goliath was tormenting King Saul's army, David was only a teenager. Saul wanted to offer him his armor and sword to go fight the giant, but David did not accept. He knew his limitations as a warrior, since he was barely a boy. Goliath would not end up being faced by David, but by God himself, because David decided not to show off but to let God work.

Later, when Saul was persecuting David because he was jealous of him, David had opportunities to stop Saul and even kill him, but he didn't because Saul was king. David never exceeded that limit, choosing to honor Saul's authority even though he had already been anointed to be the next king. The fact that David did not exceed that limit out of respect for God and the king earned him the favor of all those who followed him.

On the other hand, the story with Bathsheba was one of those in which David exceeded his limits. Bathsheba was another man's wife, and David wanted her for himself. That's why he lied, committed adultery, and became proud and blind. But the consequences of crossing the limits that God had set did not end there! David ordered the killing of Bathsheba's husband, after Bathsheba had become pregnant. He married her, but that son died shortly after birth. And finally, God did not allow David to build the temple that he had dreamed of for so long.

Crossing boundaries is never a good idea!

QUESTIONS FOR THE DISCIPLES

- Why can we trust God's limits?

- How can we help each other not to cross them?

MOBILIZE

Talking about limits with our teenagers cannot be limited to abstract or general statements. We must concretely help them establish positive boundaries in their lives to increase their freedom.

According to Drs. Henry Cloud and John Townsend, writers of the book *Boundaries*, there are several parameters that we should consider when setting concrete limits in our lives:

- In our words...

    ◊ How do you handle your language?

- With our time...

    ◊ What things do you waste time on?

- In our emotions...

    ◊ How far do we compromise our emotions?

- With people...

    ◊ Are there people who enslave you?

- In order...

    ◊ Are there areas in your life you need to order?

- In physical care...

    ◊ Have you been violent or abusive?

- With skin-to-skin contact...

  ◊ Have you crossed the limits with someone?

Raising these general questions is not to create guilt, but to protect ourselves and others. In the end, God's boundaries that we accept are like guardrails that protect us from experiencing fatal accidents and hurting others.

After helping your teens identify their areas for improvement, talk one-on-one more specifically and freely with each person, so you can help them plan personalized steps for strengthening their boundaries. Embracing with faith the truth that God's commandments are limits to protect ourselves and others gives true meaning and power to God's law.

BIBLIOGRAPHY

- Anderson, Neil. *Una vía de escape* (An escape route). Editorial Unilit. Miami, Florida. 1995.

- Arroyo, Itiel. *Amar es para valientes* (Love Is For Brave). Editorial e625. Dallas, Texas. 2018.

- Cloud, Henry and John Townsend. *Límites* (Boundaries). Editorial Vida. Mami, Florida. 2000.

- Hermosillo, Héctor. *Pastorea a tu hijo adolescente* (Shepherd Your Teenager) Editorial E625. Dallas, Texas. 2018.

- Leys, Lucas. *Diferente* (Diferent). Editorial Vida. Miami, Florida. 2015.

- Leys, Lucas. *Stamina.* Editorial e625. Dallas, Texas. 2019.

- Leys, Lucas/Burns, Jim. *El código de la pureza* (The Code of Purity). Editorial Vida. Miami, Florida. 2012.

- Leys, Lucas. *Liderazgo Generacional* (Generational Leadership). Editorial e625. Dallas, Texas. 2017.

- McDowell, Josh. *Relaciones* (Relations). Editorial Mundo Hispano. El Paso, Texas. 2007.

- McDowell, Josh. *La generación desconectada* (The Disconnected Generation). Editorial Mundo Hispano. El Paso, Texas. 2003.

- McDowell, Josh. *La verdad desnuda* (The Naked Truth). Editorial Patmos. Weston, Florida. 2011.

- Obando, Esteban; Lacota, Karen and Adrián Intrieri. *Manual de consejería para el trabajo con adolescentes* (Counseling Manual for Working with Teens). Editorial e625. Dallas, Texas. 2018.

- Pagán, Samuel and Alex Sampedro. *Credo* (Creed). Editorial e625. Dallas, Texas. 2018.

- Sampedro, Alex. *Artesano* (Craftsman). Editorial e625. Dallas, Texas. 2018.

- Townsend, John. *Límites con los adolescentes* (Boundaries With Teenagers). Editorial Vida. Miami, Florida. 2006.

- Ortiz, Félix. *Cada joven necesita un mentor* (Every Young Needs a Mentor). Editorial e625. Dallas, Texas. 2017.

- Ortiz, Félix. *Valores* (Values). Editorial e625. Dallas, Texas. 2019.

SOME QUESTIONS YOU SHOULD ANSWER:

WHO IS BEHIND THIS BOOK?

Especialidades 625 is a team of pastors and servants from different countries, different denominations, different church sizes and styles, that love Christ and the new generations.

WHAT IS E625.COM ABOUT?

Our passion is to help families and churches in Latin America to find good materials and resources for discipleship of the new generations and that is why our website serves parents, pastors, teachers, and leaders in general 365 days a year through www.e625.com with free resources.

WHAT IS PREMIUM SERVICE?

In addition to reflections and free short materials, we have a service of lessons, series, research, online books, and audiovisual resources to facilitate your task. Your church can access this service per congregation with a monthly subscription that allows all the leaders of a local church to download materials to share as a team and make the necessary copies that they find relevant for the different activities of the congregation or their families.

CAN I EQUIP MYSELF WITH YOUR HELP?

It would be a privilege to help you and with that objective we have our events and our possibilities of formal education. Visit www.e625.com/Eventos to find out about our seminars and go www.institutoE625.com to learn about the online courses offered by Instituto E 6.25

DO YOU WANT CONTINUOUS UPDATES?

Register right now for e625.com updates depending on your field of work: Children- Preteens- Teens- Young Adults.

LET'S LEARN TOGETHER!

e625.com

Downloads
suscriptions
Free
Resources
Store
Chat
Magazine
Events
Online Education
www.institutoe625.com
Seminars
Books
e625.com